Independent Reading Inside the Box

How to organize, observe, and assess reading strategies that promote deeper thinking and improve comprehension in K– 6 classrooms

Lisa Donohue

Pembroke Publishers Limited

Dedication

This book is dedicated to my children, Matthew and Hailey, who teach me more on a daily basis than I could ever dream to learn in a classroom.

© **2008 Pembroke Publishers**
538 Hood Road
Markham, Ontario, Canada L3R 3K9
www.pembrokepublishers.com

Distributed in the U.S. by Stenhouse Publishers
480 Congress Street
Portland, ME 04101
www.stenhouse.com

We acknowledge the financial support of the Government of Canada through the Book Publishing Industry Development Program (BPIDP) for our publishing activities.

We acknowledge the Government of Ontario through the Ontario Media Development Corporation's Ontario Book Initiative.

Library and Archives Canada Cataloguing in Publication

Donohue, Lisa
   Independent reading inside the box : how to organize, observe and assess reading strategies that promote deeper thinking and improve comprehension in K-6 classrooms / Lisa Donohue.

Includes index.
ISBN 978-1-55138-225-8

   1. Reading (Elementary). 2. Reading comprehension. 3. Children—Books and reading. I. Title.

LB1573.D65 2008   372.47   C2008-903369-8

Editor: Kat Mototsune
Cover Design: John Zehethofer
Typesetting: Jay Tee Graphics Ltd,

Printed and bound in Canada
9 8 7 6 5 4 3 2

Mixed Sources
Product group from well-managed forests, and other controlled sources
www.fsc.org Cert no. SW-COC-002358
© 1996 Forest Stewardship Council
FSC

Contents

Introduction

Have you ever looked at a group of students while they were reading independently? What does independent reading look like? What does it sound like? I found myself faced by this scenario not too long ago. I gazed at my students strewn around the room, some seated at their desks, some sprawled on the carpet, and others comfortably sprawled in various positions. Books in hand... open. One little girl had wedged her tiny body into a small crevice between a tall bookshelf and the classroom wall, her knees pulled to her chest and her book perched on them. A quiet hush filled the room, and I prided myself on having such a great session of independent reading well in swing. It *looked* like independent reading should, it *sounded* like independent reading should. But something was missing.

As I examined my students further, different questions began to form in my mind, questions of value, authenticity, and accountability. My thoughts changed from wondering what the readers were *doing* to what they were *thinking*. If I could somehow access their thoughts as they sat with their books, I would have a much greater insight into their learning. How could I ensure that they were actively engaged in their texts? How could I make this a time for students to effectively practice the many skills that I had been teaching through other aspects of my literacy program? Could I guide their learning when they were all reading different books? Was it possible to assess their comprehension of the material that they were reading? How could I use their independent reading books as tools to support their language acquisition and understanding of word usage? Would I actually be able to help students to identify text elements using their own independent reading books? And, finally, what could I do that would keep students engaged in their reading, and yet provide me with these valuable teaching opportunities? I didn't want to bog down my students with piles of work, and the last thing I wanted to do was trek home each week with mountains of writing to which I had to respond. I had to find a simple tool—easy to use, easy to assess, and obviously effective. The answers to these many questions were what eventually evolved into the Reading 8-Boxes introduced in this book.

The Reading 8-Box is a very versatile teaching tool that has been developed to strengthen and monitor students' comprehension of their independent reading. Reading 8-Boxes provide students with a variety of tasks intended to target a range of skills. Students are able to apply these skills to their self-selected independent reading texts, and teachers are successfully able to monitor, guide, and assess students' reading. This important tool serves to provide students with a range of graphic organizers and open-response opportunities to strengthen their thinking and responding about their books. It also gives teachers the opportunity to provide guided practice for skills, and also the tools to assess student acquisition of these skills in order to facilitate further instruction.

Reading is a complex skill set, and yet much can be accomplished with such a simple tool—eight opportunities for learning on a single page. Reading 8-Boxes contain eight individual tasks, each in its own box, in which students can record their thinking about their reading. Each task box is designed to address a different range of needs and learning styles. Hence, when eight task boxes are strategically combined into a Reading 8-Box, student engagement, focus, and progress are maximized.

Reading 8-Boxes are not reading journals.

Reading 8-Boxes differ from reading journals: in a reading journal, students and teachers write letters to each other to guide the students reading; Reading 8-Boxes provide students with a variety of focused learning activities to consider while reading. The individual tasks that make up a Reading 8-Box are open-ended, and teachers can have direct influence over what skills are being reinforced through independent reading time. Teachers have the opportunity to provide students with a range of learning experiences, and students can choose which activity to complete at each stage of their reading. Each Reading 8-Box can be individually tailored to meet the needs of individual classes and students.

Reading 8-Boxes are not book reports.

When students write book reports, they are required to have completed reading the book in its entirety before beginning to respond to its content. By the time the teacher is able to provide feedback, the student has long since moved on to another text. There is little opportunity for a teacher to monitor and guide student learning. However, Reading 8-Boxes allow teachers to assess and guide the students' learning during the reading process. The student receives regular feedback about their reading, and the teacher has regular opportunities to monitor students learning and strengthen skills as necessary.

Reading 8-Boxes are tools that provide teachers with countless opportunities to assess their students' understanding, guide their learning, and ensure that students are accountable during their independent reading time. Miriam Trehearne (2006) recommends that students read independently for 30 to 40 minutes every day. During this time, teachers are able to turn their attention to small-group instruction. The challenge, however, is making the 30 to 40 minutes of independent reading focused and purposeful, as well as building in the opportunity for accurate assessment and feedback to students. Thus, it becomes ever more important that students who are reading on their own, not directly involved in meeting with the teacher, are actively, purposefully engaged, and accountable for their learning.

1 Independent Reading and the Reading 8-Box

David Booth (2007) identifies three critical elements that all students require in order to become independent and powerful readers.

1. Choice and access: students need access to books that they can and want to read
2. Time: students need uncompromised time at home and at school to read
3. Reading Instruction: teachers need to teach students how to choose books, become powerful readers, and grow as readers.

Irene Fountas and Gay Su Pinnell (2001) state the importance of setting clear goals and expectations to help students establish and maintain positive independent reading habits. Reading is not just a busy task to occupy students' time: Reading means thinking. This includes thinking about what has been read, and thinking of oneself as a reader, so that students can move to greater independence and manage their own learning.

Fountas and Pinnell (1996) believe that teachers need to effectively manage the classroom so that they can work in a focused, uninterrupted way with small groups of children. The length of time needed for effective guided reading sessions increase as students move through the grades and texts become more complex. Thus, students not included in the ongoing small group instruction must be engaged in tasks that are substantial. Developing a strong independent-reading program seems the only logical option. When independent-reading routines are in place, with students actively engaged in learning, it then becomes easy to draw small groups of students for guided reading.

> Enabling students to effectively select and utilize Reading 8-Boxes ensures that independent reading time is purposeful and directly connected to classroom instruction.

> As the teacher works with small groups, all other students must be engaged meaningfully in literacy, and must be able to function without teacher assistance to maintain their own learning.

The Need for Independent Reading

Independent reading is the driving force in a literacy block that makes the other instructional components possible and provides opportunities for practice and reinforcement of skills learned. If students do not have the ability to work for sustained periods of time with little or no teacher involvement, it is impossible for the teacher to lead meaningful small groups. Independent reading, however, must be much more than "busy work" for the students. Students need to see their tasks as important, valid, purposeful, and worthwhile. They must also feel that their efforts will be recognized and acknowledged, and must receive further direction and instruction for their continued growth.

Students enjoy the flexibility and variety that Reading 8-Boxes present; hence, student motivation and engagement is optimized.

Setting students up for independent reading is crucial for establishing and maintaining an effective balanced literacy program with an emphasis on small-group instruction. Independent reading is the key element in balanced literacy. Although independent reading appears to occur on a daily basis without the direction of a teacher, it requires strong consistent teaching to be developed and maintained. Independent reading is the vehicle through which students are encouraged to practice the skills that we have modeled through read-alouds, discussed through shared reading, and scaffolded through guided reading. This is the students' opportunity to strengthen and reflect on these skills.

Regie Routman (2003) defines scaffolded independent-level reading as the process in which "on their own, readers choose and read books they enjoy and understand. The process is carefully monitored by the teacher." What better way to monitor this process than by providing students with a simple tool like Reading 8-Boxes to effectively strengthen and guide their learning?

The Need for Accountability

I remember a time (that does not seem like that long ago) when I was an eight-year-old child, new to the country, entering a new classroom in the month of April. The year was winding to a close, and students were well into their routines of reading and doing what I thought looked like very important work. Displayed around the room were "book worms," each with a different student's name on the face and a body that snaked along the walls. The bodies were composed of bright circles containing the titles of books that the students had read throughout the year. All at once, it became abundantly clear that everyone else's worm was of substantial length, and mine was merely a head. Desperate to discover how to add to the length of my worm, I asked for help from my new friends. They told me that all I needed to do was tell the teacher that I had read a book, and she would add a circle to the book worm bearing my name. It seemed quite simple. But how would she determine if I had *actually read* the book? Daring, brave, and desperate to have a longer book worm, I suppressed these thoughts of responsibility and swallowed hard. I approached my new teacher and informed her that I had completed my first book. Nervously, I waited for the dreaded questions to establish my accountability, but there were none. She smiled and handed me a red circle to staple onto the wall. Score! This was too easy! My worm grew, as did those of my friends—and none of us had read a single book.

My teacher no doubt had the best intentions and believed that she was accurately tracking her students' reading. She had a number of positive things in place in her classroom, such as a well-established classroom library, she provided time and motivation for her students to read, and she had implemented a creative way of tracking what the students had read. However, the fact that there was little (if any) monitoring of the students' understanding of the books they read led to the break down in the effectiveness of her reading program. Providing students with sufficient time to read during the day is important, but it is equally important that students are meaningfully engaged in their reading task, actively developing their skills, and receiving regular feedback from the teacher about their learning. As teachers, we need to constantly have our fingers on the pulse of what our students are reading, and how they are developing as readers.

Being aware of their strengths and needs provides us direction for instruction, as well as connecting with our students through the texts that they are reading.

Consider the following to support independent reading in the classroom:

1. Allowing enough time for students to become engaged in their books is essential. Students should have a set time in their schedule for independent reading that is regular and predictable. This way, students are prepared for reading time.

2. Routines should be in place so that students need to consult the teacher, thus interrupting small-group instruction, only in the event of an emergency.
   - Implement a washroom sign-out with students knowing that only one (or two) students may be in the washroom at a time. Having the sign-out in a prominent place (e.g., on the board) makes it very easy to check where someone is if they were needed or in the event of an emergency.
   - Students are permitted to use the independent reading time as a time to go to the library to choose or exchange books. In order to ensure that everyone has an equal opportunity to use the library, consider having a schedule in place. Perhaps a library sign-out posted on the board (again allowing for a very quick reference as to where all of the students are at one time) would be helpful.

No one teacher can do it all. It is important to partner with the other experts in the school.

3. A classroom library with different levels and genres of books provides choice for students to select "just right" books. However, a classroom library would never match a school library, so encourage students to take advantage of the many resources available to them in the school library. The teacher/librarian has a wealth of knowledge and is usually able to help students quickly locate books that would match their abilities and interests.

If possible, have small-group instruction in a separate corner of the classroom, rather than at a table in the centre of the room.

4. The classroom environment must be conducive to focused reading. Reading is an active process that requires that students concentrate free from distractions. If the teacher is using the independent-reading time to facilitate small-group instruction, students need to be mindful of the fact that others are reading, and conversations should be held in hushed voices so as not to distract their peers.

5. It is essential to build accountability into independent reading. This serves a number of purposes:
   - It ensures that students are on task and engaged in purposeful learning.
   - It allows for deeper individualized instruction that connects directly to small-group or classroom instruction, strengthening students' skills as they practice strategies that have been directly taught or modeled.
   - It provides opportunities to assess students' understanding of their reading and their reading strategies, and to further guide instruction.

As a teacher, it's important to have your finger on the pulse of what is new, exciting, and the hottest rage in children's literature. A teacher earns a great deal of credibility when he or she can converse intelligently with students about a popular new book or series.

6. It should be fun! Don't hesitate to share with students books you have enjoyed, or ask to borrow one that you see students reading that you think might interest you. It is also good to have students recommend books to each other.

Elements of Effective Reading Instruction

Students require very direct and clear modeling and instruction on a variety of reading techniques and strategies in order to become proficient readers. Research conducted by Michael Pressley (2002) showed that comprehension skills do not develop very well on their own; however, the comprehension strategies used by good readers can be taught, beginning with teacher explanations and modeling of the strategies, followed by scaffolded student practice of comprehension strategies during reading. A balanced reading program contains a number of elements, of which independent reading is just one.

Students' comprehension abilities depend on the instruction they receive, the quality of their literary experiences, and their ability to understand and use comprehension strategies (Block and Rodgers, 2004).

Read-Aloud

Read-alouds allow opportunities for teachers to model effective reading. Students gain experience with observing what good readers do when they are reading. Teachers should make it a practice to think aloud, encouraging students to engage with each other and with the large group while interacting with the text. Taking occasional breaks to invite comments, predictions, or connections helps to facilitate student learning and strengthen their skills.

When reading aloud to students, consider providing them with a purpose for listening prior to reading aloud to them. In this way, students become better able to filter out erroneous information and specifically target the reading strategy being taught. For example, a teacher may begin by saying, "Today while I'm reading, you need to try to use the clues from the book to determine how the main character is feeling." Assisting students by focusing their listening provides stronger awareness of reading strategies.

Introducing reading strategies through read-aloud is probably the most effective teaching technique, as it provides adequate support for students to observe a good reader at work.

Shared Reading

Shared reading provides opportunities for students to share a common reading experience with their peers or teacher. Through shared reading, the teacher models proficient reading, and the students are provided opportunities to practice together. Shared reading should not be about only the text, but the entire reading experience. Encouraging students to share their thoughts while reading provides insights into their learning.

Discussing elements such as punctuation or italicized text helps students understand the reason behind the variation in the reader's voice. For example, a teacher may say, "The author used an exclamation mark here. That means that he wanted to show a strong emotion, so let's read that with an angry voice."

Guided Reading

Guided reading provides opportunities for teachers to introduce texts that students will then read on their own. Through guided reading, the teacher sets the stage for effective reading to occur. Guided reading should include a variety of instructional techniques.

During guided reading sessions, the teacher should introduce new vocabulary and concepts that the students will encounter while reading, as well as providing guidance on how to apply reading skills and strategies that they have been taught. For example, a teacher may say, "While you're reading this next section, think about the character's motivation for his actions."

Independent Reading

In her book *Reading Essentials*, Regie Routman (2003) defines scaffolded independent-level reading as the process in which "on their own, readers choose and read books they enjoy and understand. The process is carefully monitored by the teacher."

Independent reading provides students time to practice and enjoy reading with texts of their own selection. Independent reading provides the essential time to practice reading skills and to become more adept in applying these skills to a variety of texts. Through independent reading, students gain confidence and experience as readers. Proficient readers enjoy sharing their books with others through book talks or by recommending books to a friend. Asking students to reflect on their own reading allows the teacher some insight into the student's development and it then becomes more possible to effectively tailor further instruction based on the individual student's strengths and needs.

Differences Between Silent Reading and Independent Reading

Sustained Silent Reading (Dear Time)	Scaffolded Independent Reading
Student independently chooses any book to read.	Student chooses books to read with the teacher's guidance.
Daily reading time is 10–30 minutes.	Daily reading time is at least 30 minutes.
Optional classroom library.	Classroom library is an important instructional tool.
Books may be above reading level.	Students read "just-right" books.
No monitoring by teacher.	Teacher monitors comprehension.
No writing involved.	Student keeps a reading record and writes a variety of responses to what has been read.
No instruction involved.	Instruction occurs during mini-lessons and conferences.
No reading goals are set.	Teacher and student set goals.

Adapted from Reading Essentials *by Regie Routman*

Independent reading time should range from 30 to 50 minutes of uninterrupted reading every day. Teachers should keep in mind that this is the goal and not the starting point. It is not realistic to begin the school year and expect students to be able to read for a sustained period of time without adequately preparing them for it. We need to gradually lead them in this direction and work toward the goal of increasing the duration of their reading time, while constantly monitoring their successes and challenges.

I know a young woman who recently completed an Iron Man marathon. She proudly shared that she had completed the marathon in 15 hours and 38 minutes. I stood in absolute awe of her. I could not fathom doing anything strenuous for that length of time. In fact, I probably could not have completed the last 38 minutes… let alone the previous 15 hours. However, this runner had the tools necessary to fulfill this incredible feat. How would one even begin to prepare for a challenge like this? Although this was her first Iron Man competition, she had previously run a half-Iron Man, and had spent years training in preparation for this one day. She had learned strategies to overcome the challenges she would face, and developed stamina and perseverance to "go the distance." She had found ways to maintain her focus and avoid distractions, and, in the end, the years of preparation paid off.

As teachers, we need to realize that we are training our students to reach the goal of becoming proficient readers. This is not an easy task, and certainly not one that will come about without adequate preparation. Our students are preparing for a marathon of their own. We need to provide them with the strategies to overcome challenges, the perseverance to go the distance, the focus to avoid distractions, and the skills to understand and enjoy the journey.

Remembering that independent reading is a time for students to enjoy, strengthen and develop their reading, activities should be introduced and modeled before asking students to complete the tasks on their own. Time during read-aloud or guided reading needs to be devoted to instruction on the various reading skills, so that the students are not trying to "figure out the instructions" as they are reading and trying to apply these instructions to their text.

The Reading–Writing Connection

It has become abundantly clear that the assessment of students' reading is frequently based on their ability to express their thinking about their reading with their writing. Not long ago, teachers filled their language times with establishing comprehension; all students read the same anthology of short stories and poems and then proceeded to provide responses to comprehension-based questions. Students would be required to complete multiple choice or fill-in-the-blank responses, answer short-answer questions, and occasionally provide their opinion on a text. Generally the answers were found directly in the text and savvy students could often locate italicized or bolded words that indicated where to begin looking for the correct answer. There was little, if any, differentiation of instruction—proficient readers quickly grew bored, whereas struggling readers continued to struggle. Thankfully this form of language instruction has long been regarded as less effective and literacy instruction has moved into a much more student-focused learning environment. Teachers now recognize the need for small-group learning, for targeting student interests, for direct instruction on specific reading skills and comprehension strategies, and for fostering the intrinsic motivation in students for reading.

Moving away from the comprehension-based questions was a necessary development in fostering students' love for reading and guiding them toward proficient independent reading. However, as I sat with our literacy team to discuss the most recent results of standardized testing, we noticed that students, both in our school and in our literacy network, struggled with the open-response type of questions. The reading–writing connection has weakened. Assisting students in decoding written questions and forming their responses in writing, providing evidence from the text and their own ideas to support their opinion, is necessary to build into a literacy block. It is not sufficient for students to read, enjoy, and share their books. It is essential that we revisit the skill of teaching students how to decode questions, and provide substantial answers in order to correctly represent their thinking while reading.

Teachers need to move away from questioning that focuses on the specific details of the text, and instead must provide opportunities for students to delve deeper in their understanding by responding with their writing. Instead of the

Has the pendulum swung too far away from the connection between reading and writing? Don't get me wrong… I'm far from dusting off the old readers, pulling out the blue-tinged dittos, and returning to the days of long ago. The reality is that students' understanding of their reading needs to be reflected in their ability to respond with their writing.

question "What did she do?" perhaps a question for deeper understanding may be "Justify her actions." During read-aloud, shared reading, and guided reading, students are provided with countless opportunities to share their thinking orally with their peers. Independent reading is a time for students to practice the plethora of skills that they have learned, as well as choosing texts that they truly enjoy. Providing open-ended response type questions for students to ponder while reading on their own will strengthen students' ability to share their thinking in writing about their reading.

The Reading 8-Box

A Reading 8-Box is a simple organizational tool made from a piece of paper divided into eight equal parts or boxes. In each box, students complete a different task to reflect their understanding of their reading. This resource enables teachers to address the needs of all students, targeting specific reading skills and integrating graphic organizers. The versatility of the individual task boxes enables teachers to target a wide range of learning goals. Students can work to strengthen their understanding of reading comprehension strategies, develop an awareness of text elements for a variety of text forms, develop word skills, and strengthen their comprehension. Teachers can use the format of Reading 8-Boxes to create other tasks, making them as complex or simple as necessary. Familiarizing students with the various task boxes in this book will quickly lead to independence. Following a consistent format for Reading 8-Boxes will ensure that students quickly become familiar with the structure and requirements, thus making it easy for them to follow the routine leading to independence.

It is not uncommon that, at any given moment during a literacy block, students may be participating in any one of a range of activities. It is crucial, then, that we provide tools to strengthen students' learning; just as important is the need to provide them with consistent regular feedback. If we expect our students to be independent learners, we need to give them the strategies to learn effectively. It is not sufficient for students to bury their faces in a book for 30 to 40 minutes a day. Although reading for enjoyment is important, we need to have adequate opportunities to interact with our learners, even when we are occupied with leading small groups. Unfortunately, as teachers, we are not gifted with the ability to be in multiple places at once, thus we must set up our students for independent reading prior to reading times, and provide tools like Reading 8-Boxes to guide their learning in our temporary absence.

Independent reading is critical for the structure of balanced literacy in the classroom, but it is essential for students to have this time to consolidate, practice, and enjoy the reading skills that they have been learning.

When I was a child, my parents invested possibly thousands of dollars in piano lessons over a number of years. However, as my interest veered, I eventually stopped practicing between lessons. I dreaded my weekly instructions, knowing that I was no further ahead than at my previous lesson, and this resulted in great frustration for my poor piano teacher, my parents, and me. Investing countless hours in lessons without adequate time for practice is not beneficial. Not only did I cease to play the piano after a while, but I eventually grew to dislike and resent the instrument that was the source of such frustration. We definitely do not want our students to feel this way about reading. If we continually instruct without allowing them time to explore and discover the

See pages 18–19 for a sample Reading 8-Box for a fiction text: *The Witches* by Roald Dahl.

Using 8-Boxes as a vehicle to monitor, guide, and assess students' progress provides the teacher with the opportunity to ensure that all students are meaningfully engaged.

See pages 20–21 for a sample Reading 8-Box for a non-fiction text.

wonders of the written word on their own, they, too, may grow to resent their instruments of learning.

Reading 8-Boxes provide students with the much needed time to practice, consolidate, and enjoy the skills that are actively taught during instructional portions of the literacy block. The different task boxes allow for students to apply new learning to a variety of texts that they have selected themselves. It permits them to find a purpose for new learning and strengthen their skills. Finally, it provides us with countless opportunities to assess students' learning and thinking, and, using this information, we can shape our instruction more purposefully.

Reading 8-Boxes and Reading Competencies

When we introduce our students to the concept of accountability tasks for their independent reading, it should be broken down into small manageable pieces. When Reading 8-Boxes are first introduced, we must ensure that the students are familiar with all the requirements of the tasks before they are expected to complete them on their own. Initially, consider breaking down the Reading 8-Box into individual boxes or tasks. Using direct teaching opportunities (such as read-aloud or guided reading), you can begin to familiarize students with the range of tasks. Modeling expectations during large-group instruction will allow you to help students strengthen their understanding of the requirements of some tasks. Younger children benefit from repeated practice of familiar tasks, whereas older students may need only an introduction and a brief explanation of the task requirements.

Students require very direct and clear modeling and instruction on a variety of reading techniques and strategies in order to become proficient readers themselves. Students' comprehension abilities depend on the instruction they receive, the quality of their literary experiences, and their ability to understand and use comprehension strategies.

The task boxes in this book are intended as a guide and a support for instruction, rather than a worksheet intended to replace instruction. Using the task boxes, students can apply a variety of strategies to their independent reading. These tasks are intended to support and enhance teacher guidance and instruction, not replace them. It is not intended that teachers substitute direct instruction on reading skills with worksheets, but rather that they enhance existing teaching practice with them, in order to provide opportunities for students to practice and strengthen skills that that they have been taught.

The following elements of independent reading are strengthened through the use of Reading 8-Boxes:

Active Teaching of Reading Strategies

The research clearly demonstrates that students need to be actively taught reading strategies in order to become proficient at using them. For example, Pressley (2000) states that instructions aimed at increasing comprehension abilities should focus on improving word-level competencies, building background knowledge, and establishing the use of comprehension strategies. This strategy instruction needs to become a regular component of our language instruction.

We need to use the vocabulary directly related to reading strategies and encourage our students to do likewise.

Building Stamina

Stamina is developed through regular opportunities to engage in reading. In order for students to increase their stamina, they need to have time to read every day. Initially, students may be able to actively read for only a portion of the time intended for independent reading. At the beginning of the year, teachers should teach mini-lessons, using the individual task boxes to assist students with the guidelines of independent reading time. Some students may be quite unfamiliar with reading for extended lengths of time, and genuinely unsure about what they need to do. Teachers need to set clear expectations and guidelines. We need to share with our students what independent reading looks like, sounds like, and feels like. We need to begin with short amount of time and gradually increase the duration in small increments until the students are able to maintain their reading for the desired length of time.

Maintaining Focus

Focus is maintained when students are actively engaged in their work. They need to have clear expectations, understand their tasks, and feel that their work is purposeful and important. They need to have options and choices, and receive ongoing feedback from the teacher.

Routines and Procedures

Children like routines. They like the predictability, consistency, and security that they bring. By introducing students to the routines of independent reading and the goals and requirements of Reading 8-Boxes early in the year, you enable them to quickly develop positive habits. As students become more comfortable with the routines and begin to understand the expectations, then the reading time may be gradually lengthened in order to build stamina.

Selecting Suitable Texts

See chapter 1 *Box 1: My Reading* for a more detailed look at text selection.

There are many resources that are designed to help students select appropriate books for independent reading. Students need to be able to recognize books that are appropriate for themselves independently. They should consider the level of the text, their ability to understand/comprehend it, and the subject matter of the book. Also, we need to teach students when and why it is appropriate to abandon a book. Empowering students to make successful book choices helps them feel like autonomous readers.

The Form of the Reading 8-Box

The task boxes in this book were created using a variety of sources. The tasks were designed to strengthen students' understanding of fiction and non-fiction texts, identify text features, develop and monitor word skills, and strengthen metacognitive awareness. Each task was created to target a different skill and,

Fiction 12

Roald Dahl

Illustrated by: Quentin Blake

The Witches

Character Development

Choose one character and describe the ways in which they change throughout the story. Perhaps they mature and change or learn an important lesson that affects the way they think and act.

One of the characters in the book is called child. The child was a ordinary boy, with an ordinary life, with an ordinary mother and father. But one day, his mother and father died in a crash so he had to live with his grandma. But, another day, the child became a mouse! The mouse thought like the child and acted like a child but, wasn't a child. Now, the child couldn't live long, like an ordinary child anymore.

Summarizing

Retell the story using your own words.

This book is all about bald, disgust, toe-less, evil, female witches. Once, a child lived with his mother and father, but one day, the childs parents died from a carcrash. The child lives with his grandma, and went to a hotel for the childs summer vacation. In the hotel the child found a whole bunch of witches. However, the child gets caught and turns into a mice! The child (mice) and his grandma turn all the witches into mice by a secret potion named "Number 86 delayed mousemaker." Now the child and his grandma will try to get rid of every witches in the world!

Connecting

How does your experience of a similar situation help you to understand the character's actions?

I knew how the child felt, when his parents had died from the carcrash. Both of my grandfathers had died. Both were very nice to me, but I didn't see my grandfathers too much because, my grandfather lived in Korea and I live in Canada. When the child was learned about death, he was scared to die. When I first learned about death I couldn't help myself saying "I don't want to die! I don't want to die!!!" But everyone had to face death, so there was no use.

Word Skills

Find a very descriptive passage of the book. Which words are the most effective in helping to create the imagery in your mind?

"All day long she said "My brother and I were out in the rowing boat. The whole coast is dotted with tiny islands and there's nobody on them.

Remembering

Identify and describe as many characters as possible.

Grandmamma—80 years old, smokes cigars an retired witchophile (studied witches).

The Grand High witch—Head of all witches, makes illegal money, killed another witch, very, very, very ugly.

Bruno Jenkins—Fat boy, turned into a mouse

Mr. and Mrs. Jenkins—Mother and father of Bruno, upset because Bruno turned into a mouse.

Child—Main character, turns into a mouse, mom and dad died, lives with grandmamma, loves her.

Inferring

Are there times when you can determine what a character is thinking from their words and actions? Describe one of these times. Provide evidence from the text to support your answer.

I determined that, Bruno did not care about being a mouse. I knew this because, when Bruno turned into a mouse from the grand high witch, he didn't even notice it! When Bruno was told by the child that, he was turned into a mouse like him, Bruno still didn't care, and kept on eating as he always do. I also think that Bruno is a greedy kid because when the grand high witch gave him a chocolate he took it and ate it! That's how he turned into a mice!

Visualizing

Create a magazine advertisement to promote the book. Remember to include the title, author, an illustration and an interesting caption about the book.

Febuary Issue of the [J] Magazine

Includes Posters of the book Witches

We introduce the characters!

Witches

How did he get the ideas?

See the movie. Pictures on Pg. 18

Eeech!

What are Witches? Pg. 34

Roald Dahl

Includes Biograph of Roald Dahl

Formula 86 delayed mouse maker?

19

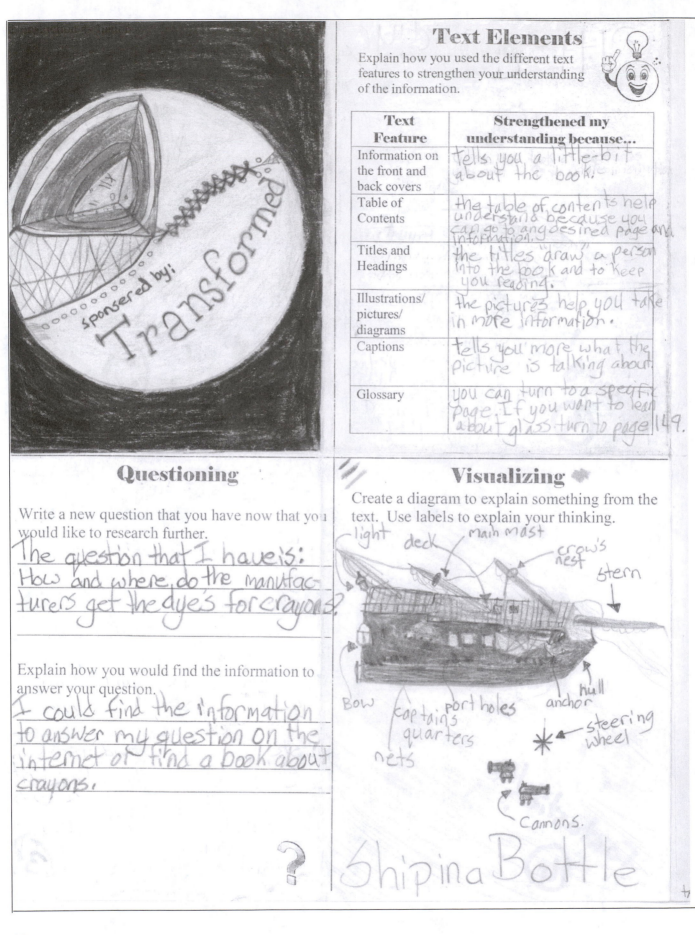

Text Elements

Explain how you used the different text features to strengthen your understanding of the information.

Text Feature	Strengthened my understanding because...
Information on the front and back covers	tells you a little-bit about the book.
Table of Contents	the table of contents help understand because you can go to any desired page and information.
Titles and Headings	the titles "draw" a person into the book and to keep you reading.
Illustrations/ pictures/ diagrams	the pictures help you take in more information.
Captions	tells you more what the picture is talking about.
Glossary	you can turn to a specific page. If you want to learn about glass turn to page 149.

Questioning

Write a new question that you have now that you would like to research further.

The question that I have is: How and where do the manufacturers get the dye's for crayons?

Explain how you would find the information to answer your question.

I could find the information to answer my question on the internet or find a book about crayons.

Visualizing

Create a diagram to explain something from the text. Use labels to explain your thinking.

light   deck   main mast   crow's nest   stern

Bow   captains quarters   port holes   anchor   hull   steering wheel

nets   Cannons.

Ship in a Bottle

Word Skills

Choose three new words. Write their definition and draw a picture to show their meaning.

Word	Definition	Picture
Slurry	a thick mixture of solid particles in a liquid such as water.	Slurry
ingot	a peice of metal that has been formed in a mold. Shaped for easy storage.	ingot
organism	an individual plant or animal	

Evaluation

Write three facts from the text and tell why each was important or interesting.

Fact #1 400 m of yarn are wound around 1 baseball.

It's interesting because: if you took 3 balls of yarn and went around a baseball dimond, it would go around it 12 times

Fact #2 In the 1800's balls bounced a lot so some games had over 100 runs.

It's interesting because: today games only have maybe 17 runs and if anyone could get 100 runs there would be 10 runs an inning

Fact #3 Did you know that 1000 "pits"(dents) on a CD can fit in this period.

It's interesting because: the pits on the CD must be so microscopic that it must be magnefied at 100x.

Determining Importance

Identify three main ideas from the text and find supporting details for each of the ideas.

Main Idea: The main idea is telling me how tea is made.
Supporting Details: first workers harvest tea leaves. Then the tea is twisted to compact it. Then the leaves are dried and chopped. Then the tea is soaked in flavorings. finally workers glue teabags over the tea so they

Main Idea: The main idea is telling me how yogurt is made.
Supporting Details: first the milk is heated to 85°. Then pistons crush fat globules. Then fruit and flavourings are added. finally the yogurt is cooled and put in a pot.

Main Idea: The main idea is telling me how jeans are made.
Supporting Details: first cotton is pressed tilty in blue dye. Then a loom forms the dyed cotton into the right shape. Then cutting machines cut the cotton to the desired size and shape. Then sewing machines sew the peices together.

Connecting

How does what you are reading now compare to what you have already read on this topic?

What I am reading now compares very well to a tv show on Discovery Chanel. The name of the tv show is, How It's Made. It tells you every step on how to make shoes, guitars and anything else you can imagine. This book also tells you every step on how it's made. For example a guitar. 1. A cutting machine cuts peices of wood to fit the right size and shape. 2. Wood struts are glued inside to improve sound. 3. The fret, nut, and saddle are glue to the bridge then the neck.

Individual tasks were created to support the development of specific reading skills as outlined in curricula expectations.

See pages 138–139 for a 11" × 17" template to make your own Reading 8-Boxes.

when combined into a Reading 8-Box, provide students with a range of learning opportunities.

When considering effective ways of combining individual task boxes into full 11" × 17" Reading 8-Boxes, it is important to ensure that there is substantial content to each set. They are certainly not "busy work," but instead provide a focused opportunity for students to strengthen their skills. There are four critical teaching elements that each Reading 8-Box should target:

- Text Elements
- Word Skills
- Taxonomy of Thinking
- Reading Comprehension Strategies

By providing a range of activities that focus specifically on these four key areas, we can help students build strong reading skills.

The first box in a Reading 8-Box is related to text selection, and helps the student identify text as "My Reading." The next three boxes in the upper tier of the Reading 8-Box each contain one box from the following areas: Text Elements, Word Skills, and Taxonomy of Thinking. Following the strong focus on reading comprehension strategies throughout literacy instruction, a typical Reading 8-Box should provide tasks to target four different reading strategies.

My Reading	Text Elements	Word Skills	Taxonomy of Thinking
Reading Strategy	Reading Strategy	Reading Strategy	Reading Strategy

11" (height) × 17" (width)

The fact that each Reading 8-Box follows the same organizational structure ensures that students easily become familiar with the format. This leads very quickly to independence.

Assessment

Examination of formal assessment pieces led to the formation of tasks that would help students become familiar with these styles of assessments and help build their capacity when taking these tests.

Task boxes are effective tools for providing immediate, accurate assessment of students' understanding of their independent reading. They allow opportunities for teachers to assess and facilitate students learning *during* the reading process.

Teachers can guide students' application of specific reading skills with ease through the selection of specific tasks. As our students are progressing as readers, their skills and needs are constantly evolving.

Using Rubrics

Monitoring students' responses to various task boxes provides us with useful information to further direct student learning. As we consider student responses, we are able to recognize areas of strength or needs. These should form the basis for future instruction. We may form groups for guided reading, or teach a mini-lesson on a particular skill that students are struggling with.

The rubrics found at the end of each chapter may be used to focus assessment of student's work. They should be used as guides for assisting students in gaining a better understanding of their strengths and areas for improvement. The ultimate goal of assessment is not to assign a mark but to aid students in becoming reflective of their work and strengthening their understanding of ways in which they can improve. Teachers can use Reading 8-Boxes as a form of formative assessment, using the data generated to guide further instruction. Using the assessment tools in this light, teachers will be able to provide direct feedback to students and assist them with setting clear goals.

See each chapter on individual task boxes for a rubric for assessment of that particular type of task.

The rubrics may be posted in the classroom or provided to students as a guide. It is not intended that every task box on every Reading 8-Box should be assessed with a separate rubric and ranked on a number of skills; this would be very time-consuming, impractical, and wasteful, expending massive amounts of paper. Instead, choose one skill as a focus. Teach to this skill, share with students how the skill will be assessed, model effective use of this specific skill, and use the rubric as a guide to collect data, form informal groupings, and further guide instruction.

Assessment for Learning

As we begin to track students' progress, it may be possible to observe individual or group trends. Tracking student's comprehension of their independent reading is valuable on so many counts. It helps us formulate a basis for further instruction, serves as an avenue for communication about texts, and aids us in monitoring our students' progress. Reading 8-Boxes not only provide accountability but are purposeful in supporting classroom learning and strengthening students' reading skills through guided practice.

See chapter 7 *Reading 8-Boxes in the Classroom,* for more on combining task boxes in response to assessment and to further learning through guided practice.

Students need specific feedback that is intended to help strengthen their skills as readers. Feedback should serve to guide their learning, rather than judge their progress. Providing anecdotal comments on students' work (rather than a mark) will help to motivate them to continue to learn and strengthen their skills. When assessing students' work, consider providing a comment that will help them to set a realistic goal. A comment like "Next time, remember to include evidence from the text to support your opinion" will provide students with clear direction for their improvement.

Students and teachers have very similar needs through the assessment process. Students need to know what their next step is in their learning process, and teachers need to know what to teach them in order to achieve this. Regular assessment followed by purposeful feedback to students will help move students forward, and using this assessment to guide instruction will ensure that our teaching is leading them along the right path.

In order to truly teach kids, we need to ensure that our assessment of student learning is the vehicle that we use to drive instruction. We need to ask ourselves, "Do we teach curriculum to kids, or do we teach kids the curriculum?" The difference is subtle, but important. Blindly striving to cover the curriculum by June will have little significance by the following September. However, if we teach our kids the strategies that they need to meet with success, monitor their progress, and teach to their needs, they will not only complete the curriculum, but actually learn it too.

2 Box 1: My Reading

How students select books and evaluate books they have read tells us a great deal about their thinking. As teachers, we have many questions around the ways in which our students select books. Are students reading a variety of genres of books? Have they sampled books from a range of authors? Do they select books that are challenging but not too difficult? Do they take risks as readers and explore new styles? Have they learned when and why it is suitable to abandon a book?

Helping Students Select Texts

Boushey and Moser (2006) teach students the acronym I PICK to support them while making book selections:
I choose a book.
Purpose: Why do I want to read it?
Interest: Does it interest me?
Comprehend: Am I understanding what I am reading?
Know: I know most of the words.

There are many resources that are designed to help students select appropriate books for independent reading. Students need to be able to recognize books that are appropriate for themselves independently. They should consider the level of the text, their ability to understand/comprehend it, and the subject matter of the book. Also, we need to teach students when and why it is appropriate to abandon a book. Empowering students to make successful book choices helps them feel like autonomous readers.

One Text vs. Many

Especially for younger students, the My Reading box could provide space to create an illustration to represent the text or texts, and to include as much detail as they wish. Students relish the opportunity to create a beautiful, detailed cover for their work.

Younger readers read many short books in the same time that an older reader would read one longer book. Therefore, the expectations that we place on these students need to be very different. In a junior classroom, most students are reading longer texts as their independent reading books; it would make sense that these students would use the same text to complete one complete Reading 8-Box. This way they may finish most if not all of the eight activities using the same book.

The purpose of the task boxes is to monitor student's understanding of their reading, not make their reading monotonous or tedious. If younger students were required to complete all eight boxes for one short, leveled reading book, they would spend the majority of their reading time…well, not reading. Young readers need to read, read, read, and pause occasionally to respond. In fact, this should be the case for all readers. The tasks that we ask them to complete should not dominate their time. Young readers may read a number of short texts before they are able to complete a full Reading 8-Box. Although we are guiding their learning and monitoring their understanding, we need to ensure that the students maintain control over their text selection, and the primary purpose of reading time remains reading.

Understanding what draws students to specific texts will enable us to better guide their choices, target their interests, and strengthen their motivation to read. As teachers, we need to guide their text selection to ensure that they are choosing texts that are of appropriate difficulty and that contain suitable content. Many young readers may need the excitement of high-interest/low-vocabulary texts in order to strengthen their fluency and understanding of texts; stronger readers may need guidance when selecting young adult texts, as the content may contain more mature themes. As we gain a greater understanding of the processes that students use to select texts we can identify with their selections and more effectively guide their choices.

When selecting texts, reflective readers continually revisit strategies that result in success. Gaining some insight into readers' text selection allows teachers to guide students selections in order that they will enjoy their choices, meet with success, and inevitably become proficient at monitoring these strategies independently.

This sample task box is for the non-fiction text *The Boys' Book: How to be the Best at Everything* by Dominique Enright and Guy Macdonald.

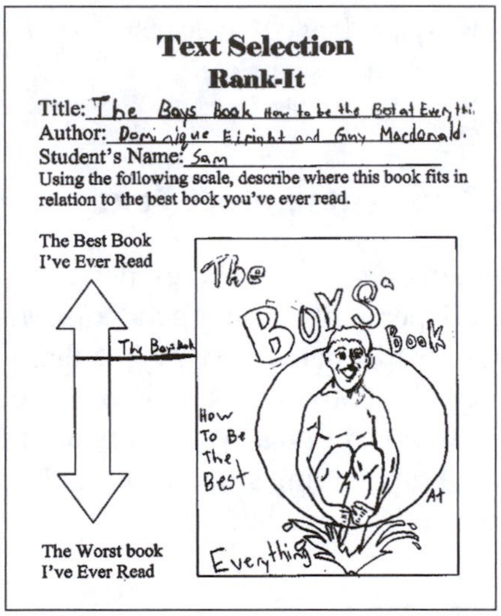

The task box shown here allows students to rank the book they are currently reading. The ranking of the book provides some insight into the reader's perception of the book. Should the book be ranked high, the student may be interested to read other books by the same author, about the same topic, or on a related theme. If, however, the book is ranked low, this would indicate a lot about the way the student is responding to their book selection. Perhaps it is too easy or, more likely, too challenging; perhaps the reader is not connecting with the subject matter or the author.

Text Selection Task Descriptions

The reproducible boxes on page 28 can be copied and placed into Reading 8-Boxes for students' use.

Teachers can gain a better insight into their student's choice around reading using these task boxes.

Rank It

Title: _____
Author: _____
Student's Name: _____

Recommendation

Title: _____
Author: _____
Student's Name: _____

Why did you choose this book?

_____
_____
_____

I Love It Because ...

Title: _____
Author: _____
Student's Name: _____

After reading, I was glad I chose this book because

_____
_____

Initial Attraction

Title: _____
Author: _____
Student's Name: _____

After reading this book, I want my next book to be

_____
_____

RANK IT

This task provides students with the opportunity to rank their current book with other books that they have read. Using the scale, they plot where this book fits in comparison to the best book they've ever read and the worst book they've ever read. The large box provides adequate space for students to create a detailed illustration of the text, perhaps an image that would make an exciting cover or demonstrate the most important event in the text.

RECOMMENDATION

In this task box, students describe their rationale for selecting this book and consider an audience who would particularly enjoy it. Readers may choose to recommend the book to a specific person (like a best friend) or a group of people (kids who like baseball). They may indicate that the book is suitable for a younger or older audience, or people with specific interests. The large box invites readers to illustrate a part of the text they think is the most important. Some students may include words, phrases, or sentences to describe what their picture is representing.

I LOVE IT BECAUSE...

In this task, readers are asked to think of the reasons that they enjoyed this book. They are then provided the opportunity to reflect on their choice and consider whether they would like to read a book with a similar theme, topic, or author. Student responses to these questions may indicate to teachers an interest in a particular topic or a special connection with a new author. Again, a large box is provided for students to create an illustration of an important/favorite part of the text. Some readers may choose to explain reasons that they did not enjoy the book; in this way, they are also effectively demonstrating their preferences of texts. This information is just as valuable when helping students select other books.

INITIAL ATTRACTION

This task box invites readers to recall their initial reasons for selecting the text. They are also asked to consider the ways in which this book will influence their next book choice. A reader who enjoyed the book or connected with it some way would be very likely to wish to read another book that has similar features. Likewise, if the student did not particularly enjoy the book, this too will affect their next text selection. As the student recalls the strategies initially used to select the text, he or she will repeat them, refine them, or learn from them in some way.

Rank It

Title:_____

Author:_____

Student's Name:_____

Using the following scale, describe where this book fits in relation to the best book you've ever read.

The Best Book I've Ever Read

The Worst Book I've Ever Read

Recommendation

Title:_____

Author:_____

Student's Name:_____

Why did you choose this book?

_____

_____

Who do you think would enjoy this book? Why?

_____

_____

I Love It Because ...

Title:_____

Author:_____

Student's Name:_____

After reading, I was glad I chose this book because

_____

_____

Would you choose a book by the same author or on the same theme again? Why?

_____

Initial Attraction

Title:_____

Author:_____

Student's Name:_____

After reading this book, I want my next book to be

_____

_____

What initially attracted you to this book?

_____

3 Box 2: Elements of Text

What guides our familiarity with a wide range of text forms? How is it so easy for us, as adult readers to recognize each text form at a glance, and have the strategies with which to approach them?

Take a moment and reflect on the number of text forms you are exposed to on a daily basis. In my world, the newspaper magically arrives at my house every day, in addition to the variety of flyers, bills, and other mail. The Internet rapidly delivers messages and images from unknown strangers as well as e-mails from friends, family, and work associates. Our children's picture books are piled precariously on coffee tables and bookshelves. Professional reading books, articles, and magazines lay scattered around my desk, and the latest fashion magazine is crushed under the weight of a novel that I promised myself time to enjoy. Amazingly, it is easy to recognize these text forms as uniquely different in their purpose and content. Glancing through the newspaper, it becomes very clear which articles are worthy of my time. The index or table of contents guides me to the information I am seeking in the professional books, and the images and captions of the fashion magazine dictate which articles I will pursue. The novel however, must be read sequentially—I begin at the beginning and end at the end.

As readers, we are unconsciously aware of the fact that we can recognize the different elements of texts, and automatically know how to make sense of them. We use the headlines of newspapers, the captions of images in magazines, the glossary of a text—and we do it strategically and intuitively. We recognize the elements of different texts and the purposes they serve in helping us to better understand or access the information.

Children need instruction in order to learn the purpose of each element and ways in which to use them effectively. They need to be taught the variety of ways in which we can approach different texts. They need to know that some texts need to be read sequentially, and some can be read in any order.

Non-Fiction Texts

The task boxes for text elements are grouped into fiction and non-fiction. There are a few instances where a task is suitable for either text form, but generally it is better to create genre-specific Reading 8-Boxes (fiction and non-fiction).

As teachers, we need to expose children to a variety of non-fiction texts and demonstrate strategies with which to approach them. Non-fiction texts have elements that are very different from their fictional counterparts. Many non-fiction texts are non-continuous and can be read out of sequence. Specific skills that we need to teach students include

- learning about tables of contents and indexes to locate specific information
- using a glossary to determine the meaning of unfamiliar terms
- using captions to interpret images
- using images to strengthen their understanding of the text.

- understanding chapter titles and subheadings as mental organizers
- using lists as summarizing tools for important information
- distinguishing between facts and opinions

Text Elements

Explain how you used the different text features to strengthen your understanding of the information.

Text Feature	Strengthened my understanding because...
Information on the front and back covers	It gives you a simple overview of the book.
Table of Contents	It gave me a quick way to find important information.
Titles and Headings	They tell you what each page is about.
Illustrations/ pictures/ diagrams	They give you a visual understanding of what things look like.
Captions	The captions tell you what is in the picture
Glossary	It helps you understand strange/new words mean.

Consider the sample task box shown here. It is intended to help strengthen understanding of non-fiction text elements. Students are asked to examine six common non-fiction elements and describe ways in which they helped to strengthen their understanding of the text. Students are not asked to reflect on the elements in isolation, but rather to develop an understanding of their purpose in the text and the ways in which they are important. This task gives the teacher some insight into a student's thinking about each text feature, and serves as a good indicator of their ability to monitor their comprehension as well.

Fiction Texts

The elements of fiction texts seem somewhat more familiar to students. Perhaps it is due to the fact that most young children are introduced to stories well before they begin their formal schooling. We teach them about character, setting, and plot at an early age. They learn to identify fiction elements in the writing of others and, as young authors, include them in their own stories. As children continue to develop, we need to ensure that their understanding of fiction elements becomes progressively deeper. They should learn about character and plot development, conflict and resolution, motivation and climax. They should consider a variety of settings, the choices made by the author, and the alternative perspectives posed by different characters.

The three sample task boxes shown on page 31 describe some familiar fiction text elements: setting, plot, characters. In each of these tasks, students are asked to reflect on the specific text feature and provide evidence for their thinking. They may need to write a sentence or phrase using their own ideas, or provide a quote from the text to support their thinking. The open-ended nature of the tasks allows for versatility, and students of different levels will complete the same task in very different ways.

On page 31, The Setting task is on the fiction text *The City Underground* by Suzanne Martel; the Plot Graph is on *The Watsons Go to Birmingham–1963* by Christopher Paul Curtis; the Characters task is on *Rover Saves Christmas* by Roddy Doyle.

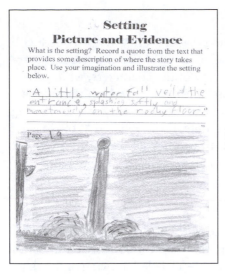

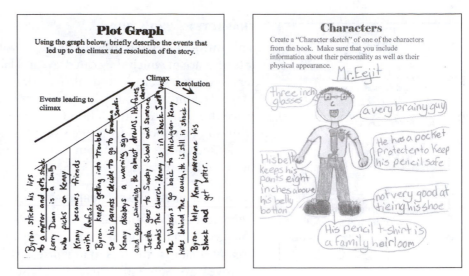

When assembling Reading 8-Boxes, keep in mind the important aspect of understanding the various text elements. Each Reading 8-Box should contain one task box that focuses on text elements.

The following descriptions are intended to help teachers choose appropriate tasks that will best strengthen students' skills. Each task description refers to a specific box and outlines briefly the purpose and intent of each activity. The boxes are introduced in a sequential manner, beginning with the simplest tasks and becoming increasingly complex.

The reproducible boxes on pages 36–40 can be copied and placed into Reading 8-Boxes for students' use.

The first set of task boxes are designed to familiarize students with the various elements in text. Initially, elements are presented individually, and later combined together as students become more familiar with text elements.

Text Elements Task Descriptions: Fiction

Setting
Picture and Sentence

Where does the story take place. Draw a picture and write a sentence to describe the setting.

SETTING: PICTURE AND SENTENCE

In this task, students describe the setting using pictures and words. Young readers may be able to provide a detailed illustration of where the story takes place and include a descriptive sentence to accompany it. Students should be encouraged not only to identify the setting but also to describe it as vividly as possible. Invite readers to include descriptive terms—"dark," "squeaky," "bright," "loud," "musty," etc.—to accurately reflect the setting of the story.

Setting
Picture and Evidence

What is the setting? Record a quote from the text that provides some description of where the story takes place. Use your imagination and illustrate the setting below.

SETTING: PICTURE AND EVIDENCE

This task box stresses the importance of providing evidence from the text. Students record a quote from the text that provides some description of the setting of the story. They are then encouraged to use their imagination to illustrate the setting based on the quote. Readers need to be aware of the need to support their ideas by referring to the text. As students become familiar with providing evidence for their answers, they will formulate stronger responses.

**Characters
Who's Who?**

Who are the important characters in the story? Draw and label a picture of each of them.

**Character Development
(primary)**

Choose one character from the story. Describe what this character was like at the beginning of the story, and what he/she was like at the end.

Beginning	End

**Character Development
(junior)**

Choose one character and describe the ways in which this character changes throughout the story. Perhaps he/she matures or learns an important lesson that affects the way he/she thinks and acts.

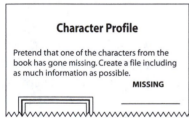

Character Profile

Pretend that one of the characters from the book has gone missing. Create a file including as much information as possible.

MISSING

Character Sketch

Create a character sketch of one of the characters from the book. Make sure that you include information about the character's personality as well as physical appearance.

CHARACTERS: WHO'S WHO?

This introductory task is well suited for young readers. They are provided with lots of space in which they can draw and label pictures of the important characters in the story. Some students may draw many of the characters, while others may select only a few. It is interesting to observe the way in which the students place the characters in relation to each other and whether they are interacting with other characters from the story; for example, is the Big Bad Wolf chasing Little Red Riding Hood around the room, or are they all drawn in a row, or presented more randomly?

CHARACTER DEVELOPMENT (PRIMARY)

The chart allows students to consider ways in which the character may have changed from the beginning of the story to the end. The openness of the graphic organizer allows students to organize and present their thinking in a number of creative ways. Some students may choose to create a labeled drawing of the character in both boxes; others may choose to use words, sentences, and evidence from the text to support their thinking. Evidence may be presented in the form as an example from the story or a direct quote from the text.

CHARACTER DEVELOPMENT (JUNIOR)

This open-response task invites students to consider ways in which one character has changed throughout the story. Readers may think about important lessons the character may have learned, ways the character has grown and matured, and important ways the character's life has changed. In this task, students will begin to connect ideas from the beginning of the text with information found in later sections. As students form these connections, they will begin to see the story in a more complete way, strengthening their understanding of the character's journey throughout the text.

CHARACTER PROFILE

Creating a profile of one character encourages students to analyze the information in the text in a creative way. In this task, they are to pretend that one of the characters from the book has gone missing. They must create a missing-person file. Students will combine information from the text with their own imagination to provide as much information as possible.

CHARACTER SKETCH

Readers create a character sketch for one of the characters in the text. The character sketch may contain an illustration that is supported by descriptive text. Some students may choose to create a diagram-like drawing with captions describing specific elements of the character's appearance and personality. Others may choose to include a paragraph of descriptive writing to support their picture.

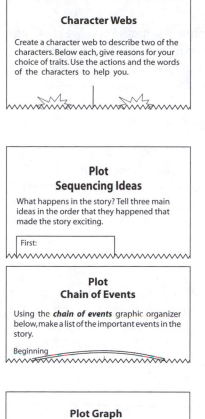

Character Webs

Create a character web to describe two of the characters. Below each, give reasons for your choice of traits. Use the actions and the words of the characters to help you.

Plot
Sequencing Ideas

What happens in the story? Tell three main ideas in the order that they happened that made the story exciting.

First:

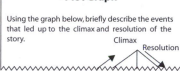

Plot
Chain of Events

Using the **chain of events** graphic organizer below, make a list of the important events in the story.

Beginning

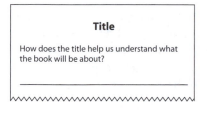

Plot Graph

Using the graph below, briefly describe the events that led up to the climax and resolution of the story.

Climax

Resolution

Title

How does the title help us understand what the book will be about?

Title Choice

Why do you think the author selected the title for the story?

CHARACTER WEBS

Students create webs to describe two characters from the text. Using the graphic organizer, students may respond using pictures, symbols, words, or phrases to convey as much information as possible. Under each web, readers are asked to give reasons for their choice of character traits. They should use evidence from the text that supports their thinking by showing the actions, thoughts, or words of the character.

PLOT: SEQUENCING IDEAS

Students select three main ideas from the story and describe them in the correct sequence. Some students may reflect on the text as a whole and focus on the beginning, middle, and end; others might select one important event and describe three things that occurred during this selection. Students provide pictures, words, sentences, and evidence from the text to help explain their ideas.

PLOT: CHAIN OF EVENTS

The graphic organizer invites readers to examine the impact that one event may have on subsequent events. Students record four sequential events from the story and reflect on the ways in which one event leads to the next. Encourage students to reflect on the interdependence of the various plot components and think about the result if one of the events had occurred differently or not at all.

PLOT GRAPH

In this chart, students graph the various events in the text that lead to the climax of the story. They may notice that events become increasingly intense and exciting as the rising actions lead to the climax. Following the climax, the story is usually resolved with falling action ending in the resolution. This task box should be completed on an ongoing basis throughout reading the text, so that students can refer to the chart as the plot builds throughout the story. Students may summarize each significant event with one sentence in order to fit the necessary information onto the chart.

TITLE

This introductory task encourages students to think about the author's choice of a title and how it helps us understand the content of the book. At the beginning, students use the title to predict what they may learn from the text; later they may refer to the title as a clue to determine what the author thought was important in the text. Often the significance of a title becomes clear once the reader has a greater understanding of the book as a whole.

TITLE CHOICE

Students think about reasons why the author selected the title for the story. They need to provide examples from the text that show why the title was a good choice for the book. This activity helps readers to see the book in its entirety and to think about some of the decisions made by the author.

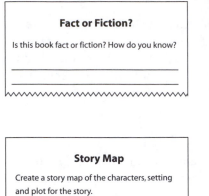

Fact or Fiction?

Is this book fact or fiction? How do you know?

FACT OR FICTION

Deciphering the difference between fact and fiction is sometimes more challenging than it may seem. Readers consider evidence in the text that helps them to conclude that the text is either fact or fiction. Some students may consider various text elements that are characteristic of certain text forms; others may provide concrete examples of information presented in the writing that clearly illustrates the nature of the text.

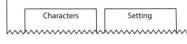

Story Map

Create a story map of the characters, setting and plot for the story.

| Characters | Setting |

STORY MAP

This story map allows students to think about the characters, setting, and plot. The plot is divided into the beginning, middle, and end. Using the graphic organizer, students may use a variety of creative ways to respond to this task. With more complex books, it may be necessary for students to select the most important information to include in each of the boxes.

Cover Information

What information on the front and covers help you to predict what the book will be about?

COVER INFORMATION

"Never judge a book by its cover" may be a familiar adage, but effective readers rely on cover information to make important decisions about the content of a book. In this task, students use the information on the front and back covers to formulate predictions about what they think the text will be about. They may refer to information that they have encountered while reading that support the ideas they had from their initial examination of the covers.

Text Elements Task Descriptions: Non-Fiction

Titles, Labels, Pictures

Look through the book. Find and record examples of titles, labels, and pictures.

Title:_____ page _____

TITLES, LABELS, PICTURES

This task introduces young readers to some of the text features in non-fiction texts. Readers identify examples of titles, labels, and pictures that they encountered while reading.

Strengthening Understanding (primary)

Complete the chart below describing how each of these elements helped you to understand the text.

STRENGTHENING UNDERSTANDING (PRIMARY)

In this task, readers consider three non-fiction elements (table of contents, index, and illustrations) and describe ways in which they helped to strengthen their understanding of the content of the text. Students may describe ways in which they used the different elements to locate specific facts, explain information that they learned, or describe ways in which their understanding of a specific fact was clarified using one of the text elements (e.g., using a diagram to understand the water cycle).

Strengthening Understanding (junior)

Explain how you used the different text features to strengthen your understanding of the information

STRENGTHENING UNDERSTANDING (JUNIOR)

This task box focuses on a similar skill set to that in the previous task. In this task readers consider the following text elements: cover information, table of contents, titles and headings, illustrations/pictures/diagrams, captions, and glossary. Students may describe ways in which they used the text feature to locate specific information or strengthen their understanding of the text.

NEW ILLUSTRATIONS

Illustrations, diagrams, and pictures bring a lot of meaning to non-fiction texts. They assist readers to visualize concepts, they support new ideas, and they illustrate different terminology. In this task, students create four new illustrations that could be added to their book. They are reminded of the importance of including a caption to clarify their illustrations. Encourage students to create new and unique pictures rather than copying existing ones from the text.

Setting
Picture and Sentence

Where does the story take place. Draw a picture and write a sentence to describe the setting.

_____

_____

_____

Setting
Picture and Evidence

What is the setting? Record a quote from the text that provides some description of where the story takes place. Use your imagination and illustrate the setting below.

" _____

_____

_____ "

Page_____

Characters: Who's Who?

Who are the important characters in the story? Draw and label a picture of each of them.

Character Development
(primary)

Choose one character from the story. Describe what this character was like at the beginning of the story, and what he/she was like at the end.

Beginning	End

Character Development (junior)

Choose one character and describe the ways in which this character changes throughout the story. Perhaps he/she matures or learns an important lesson that affects the way he/she

_____

_____

_____

_____

_____

_____

_____

_____

Character Profile

Pretend that one of the characters from the book has gone missing. Create a file including as much information as possible.

MISSING

Recent Picture

Name: _____

Age: _____

Last seen at the following location:

_____

_____

Description: _____

_____

_____

_____

_____

Character Sketch

Create a character sketch of one of the characters from the book. Make sure that you include information about the character's personality as well as physical appearance.

Character Webs

Create a character web to describe two of the characters. Below each, give reasons for your choice of traits. Use the actions and the words of the characters to help you.

_____

_____

_____

_____

_____

_____

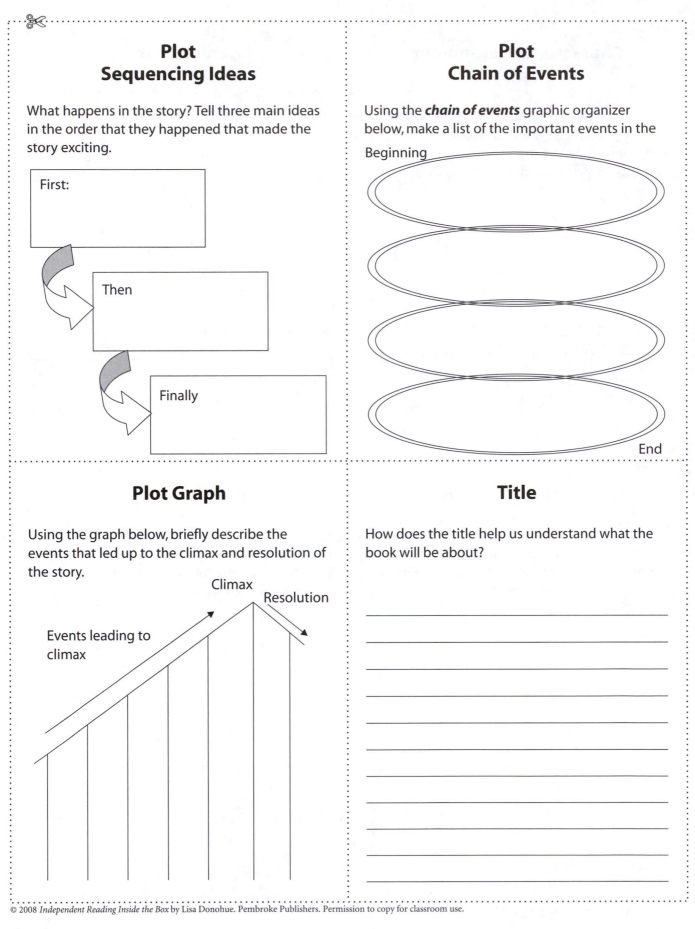

Plot
Sequencing Ideas

What happens in the story? Tell three main ideas in the order that they happened that made the story exciting.

First:

Then

Finally

Plot
Chain of Events

Using the **chain of events** graphic organizer below, make a list of the important events in the

Beginning

End

Plot Graph

Using the graph below, briefly describe the events that led up to the climax and resolution of the story.

Climax

Resolution

Events leading to climax

Title

How does the title help us understand what the book will be about?

_____

_____

_____

_____

_____

_____

_____

_____

_____

_____

_____

Title Choice

Why do you think the author selected the title for the story?

_____

_____

_____

_____

Give an example from the text that shows why the title was a good choice for this book.

_____

_____

_____

_____

_____

_____

Fact or Fiction?

Is this book fact or fiction? How do you know?

_____

_____

_____

_____

_____

_____

_____

_____

_____

_____

Story Map

Create a story map of the characters, setting and plot for the story.

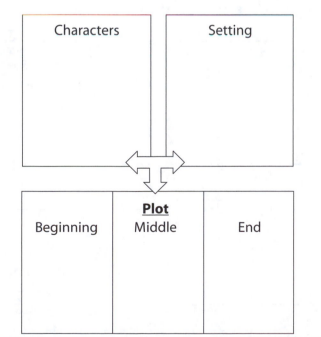

Characters	Setting

Plot

Beginning	Middle	End

Cover Information

What information on the front and back covers help you to predict what the book will be about?

_____

_____

_____

_____

_____

_____

_____

_____

_____

_____

Titles, Labels, Pictures

Look through the book. Find and record examples of titles, labels, and pictures.

Title:_____ page _____

Title:_____ page _____

Label:_____ page _____

Label:_____ page _____

Picture of:_____ page _____

Picture of:_____ page _____

_____

_____

_____

Strengthening Understanding (primary)

Complete the chart below describing how each of these elements helped you to understand the text.

Text Element	How they helped
Table of Contents	
Index	
Illustrations Pictures Diagrams	

Strengthening Understanding (junior)

Explain how you used the different text features to strengthen your understanding of the information.

Text Feature	Strengthened my understanding because ...
Information on the front and back covers	
Table of Contents	
Titles and Headings	
Illustrations/ Pictures/ Diagrams	
Captions	
Glossary	

New Illustrations

Create four new illustrations to support the information in the text. Remember to include a caption for each illustration.

Rubric for Text Elements

Skill	Level 1	Level 2	Level 3	Level 4
Identify and describe elements of text	Student is beginning to name and locate the various text elements but may have difficulty describing their features or purpose.	Student is able to name, locate, and describe some of the various text elements.	Student is able to name, locate, and describe most of the various text elements.	Student is able to name, locate, and describe all of the various text elements.
Use text elements to enrich understanding of text	Student is rarely able to describe ways in which the different text elements contribute to his/her understanding of the text.	Student is beginning to describe ways in which the different text elements contribute to his/her understanding of the text.	Student is able to describe ways in which the different text elements contribute to his/her understanding of the text.	Student is able to thoroughly describe a variety of ways in which the different text elements contribute to his/her understanding of the text.
Demonstrate an understanding of plot development	Student is able to describe a few of the events from the text; these events may be irrelevant or minor to the plot as a whole.	Student is able to describe some of the sequential events that formed the key elements of the plot.	Student is able to describe the sequential events that formed the key elements of the plot.	Student is able to describe the sequential events that formed the key elements of the plot; has a good understanding of how these events combine to form the plot (conflict and resolution).
Demonstrate an understanding of character development	Student is beginning to describe a few of the ways in which characters change throughout a book; evidence is lacking.	Student is able to describe some of the ways in which characters change throughout a book; evidence provided may be weak or irrelevant.	Student is able to describe the ways in which characters change throughout a book and can provide evidence to support his/her thinking.	Student is able to thoroughly describe the ways in which characters change throughout a book and can provide critical evidence to support his/her thinking.

4 Box 3: Word Skills

Language acquisition is a natural process, as young children learn new words and integrate them into their existing vocabulary. They automatically generate meanings and figure out ways to use them effectively through trial, error, and gentle guidance from adults in their lives.

Young readers also have an innate ability to construct meaning for unfamiliar words. There is no better example of this than the effect J.K. Rowling's world of Harry Potter has had on young readers. Fans of the books easily make sense of new words, and even become adept at translating the Latinate language. Ask any avid Harry Potter reader, and he or she will be able to define words like *horcruxes, muggle, parselmouth,* or *dementor,* and explain incantations like "Wingardium Leviosa" or "Petrificus Totalus." Readers have become fluent with this "Potter language" and are comfortable integrating its meaning into their existing knowledge. How do our young readers generate definitions for literally hundreds of these non-English words? There is no need for children to look these terms up in a dictionary to confirm their meaning, as they have been able to generate an understanding of the words from the context with which they have been read. A new word is integrated into one's existing vocabulary through repeated exposure in meaningful contexts.

As we guide our children through their reading, we should be mindful of this natural process and strive to support it, rather than act against it. Presenting children with long lists of vocabulary out of context will not assist them in bringing meaning to these words the next time they encounter them. Using task boxes to record words that are new to them (rather than what *we think* will be new to them) gives students a much more personal connection to the text being read. As our readers discover new words, we need to help them use the context cues to determine meaning, and confirm or correct as necessary.

In the first sample on page 43, the student selected a descriptive passage from the text (in this case, Jack London's *Call of the Wild*) and represented the image that was brought to mind. The student went on to identify which words were most effective in conveying these images. Asking readers to think of words in context is more likely to help them successfully generate meaningful understandings than presenting words in isolation.

The second task on page 43 asks the student to identify parts of speech through the reading; the text here is *Inkspell* by Cornelia Funke. Students can successfully identify various parts of speech in the context of a book. This way, they not only become familiar with the words, but develop an awareness of their correct usage.

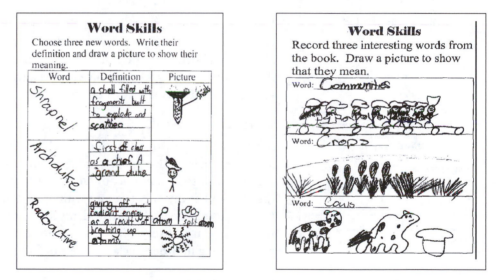

These samples show how task boxes can be helpful when students are reading non-fiction selections and encounter new vocabulary. In both tasks, students record three words that are new to them and represent the meaning of each. Using context cues in addition to the dictionary to record the meaning of new words helps students learn to use the dictionary more effectively, in addition to adding to their vocabulary.

For the non-fiction tasks, the texts were *The Trenches* by Jim Eldridge and *All About Canadian Communities: Farming Communities*.

The reproducible boxes on pages 47–51 can be copied and placed into Reading 8-Boxes for students' use.

Word Skills Task Descriptions

The following tasks are designed to strengthen students' vocabulary and word skills. Some tasks are intended to encourage students to attend to new and interesting vocabulary, some introduce students to various parts of speech, and others help students to develop an understanding of new words using a variety of resources (dictionaries, thesaurus, etc.).

When combining individual tasks to form a Reading 8-Box, one task should be dedicated to strengthening students' word skills. Because students encounter new words in all text forms (fiction and non-fiction), the task boxes presented here are suitable for both text types.

Three Words and Pictures

Record three interesting words from the book. Draw a picture to show what they mean.

Six Words and Pictures

Write some new words that you learned while reading. Draw a picture to show what they mean.

Word Collector

Become a **word collector** of interesting and unique words. How many words can you have in your word sack?

Alphabetical Order

Record five interesting words from the book.

1. _____

2. _____

Word Search

Create a word search about the story using character names, place names, and new vocabulary you have learned. Share it with a friend.   **Word List**

Initial Sound

Find pairs of words that have the same beginning sound (for example, **br**ight and **br**own)

Adjectives

How many adjectives (describing words) can you find? For example: *big brown* bear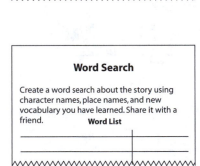

THREE WORDS AND PICTURES

In this task box, students record interesting words they encounter while reading and represent each word with an illustration. Readers are encouraged to use the illustration to demonstrate their understanding of the meaning of each word. Some students may wish to include a phrase that helps clarify the meaning of the word or connects the word to their reading. Encourage readers to indicate the number where the word was found, so that you can clarify any misconceptions and support the student's contextual understanding of the word.

SIX WORDS AND PICTURES

Similar to the previous task, readers are provided with six places in which they can identify new words and illustrate their meanings with pictures. Again, it is important for students to include the page number so you can reinforce the word's meaning in the context of the book.

WORD COLLECTOR

How many words can you collect? Students start a word collection of unique or interesting words. They can use their "word sack" as a place to keep and add to their word collection. Encourage students to record the page number where the word was found. When conferencing with students, you can refer to the text and assist students in developing a meaning and context for their special words.

ALPHABETICAL ORDER

While reading, students record five new, unique, or interesting words they encounter. Once they have selected five words, they reorganize the words into alphabetical order. Conferencing about this task gives you an opportunity to discuss the author's word choice and ensure that students have a good understanding of the various word meanings.

WORD SEARCH

Students create a word search using character names, places, and new vocabulary from their books. Spelling is critical in this task, as misspelled words will be very difficult to locate. Encourage students to carefully record their words from the text and, if unsure about a spelling, to double check with the book or a dictionary. It may be useful for students to record the page number beside any new words they are unsure of; this way the text can be quickly referenced during conferencing in order to clarify the word meaning and usage.

INITIAL SOUND

In this task, students look for pairs of words that have the same initial sound or consonant blend. Some readers record more than two words with each initial sound. This task may be more challenging than it looks, especially if students are attempting to locate words that begin with blends (e.g., *br–*). If students are having difficulty identifying words with similar initial sounds, it can help if you give them a selection of common starting sounds to search for (e.g., *th–, sh–, ch–*).

ADJECTIVES

Adjectives are words that are used to create vivid images in reader's minds. We rely on these words in order to visualize what we read. Adjectives are possibly one of the first parts of speech that young readers become familiar with. They are able to think of adjectives as describing words. In this task box, students record as many adjectives as possible from their reading. Later, students can use the list of adjectives as a resource to use to enrich their own writing.

VERBS IN ACTION

Young readers like to think of verbs as action words. How better to represent an action word than with a picture of someone or something performing that action? Students select four verbs from their reading and create an illustration that shows the verb in action. When conferencing with students, take this opportunity to discuss various verb tenses and irregular verbs.

NOUNS

Simple nouns (people, places, and things) are everywhere. In this task box, young readers record as many examples of nouns as they can find in their books. Some readers may be aware of the difference between simple nouns and proper nouns; if not, this may be a focus for a mini-lesson or conference.

ADJECTIVES, VERBS, AND NOUNS

These three basic parts of speech become quite familiar for younger readers. This activity invites students to select one page from their book and record as many examples of adjectives, verbs, and nouns as they are able to identify. Many young students will include adverbs in the category of adjectives, which may become a focus for a mini-lesson or even large-group lesson.

ADVERBS

In this task box, students are provided with the definition of an adverb and must locate pairs of verbs and adverbs. Seeing the connection between the adverb and action it is describing will help students have a stronger understanding of these parts of speech.

ADJECTIVES AND ADVERBS

Many students find the differentiation between adjectives and adverbs clear in theory, but find it much more challenging when looking at words in context. With this task, it is important for students to remember that the adverb describes the verb. It may be helpful for students who are having difficulty with this task to include the verb that the adverb is describing.

WORD CHOICE

Recognizing and appreciating an author's word choice helps students begin to integrate these words into their own vocabulary. In this activity, students record a very descriptive passage of the book and identify the words that are most effective in helping to create a mental image. Readers are given the opportunity to express their thinking in a very open-ended activity. Many students will seize the opportunity to create an illustration to support the passage that they selected from the text.

NEW TO ME

Readers select three words that are new and interesting. They can then use a dictionary to find and record the definition. Finally, students create an illustration for each word that demonstrates its meaning. During conferences, ensure that students have selected the appropriate definition for each word based on the

---

Verbs in Action

Verbs are action words (*run, twist, fly* and *crawl*). Write some verbs from your book and illustrate the action they represent.

Nouns

A **noun** is a person, place, or thing. How many different kinds of nouns can you find in the book?

Adjectives, Verbs, and Nouns

Pick one page in the book. How many adjectives, nouns, and verbs can you find on this one page? Write them below:

Adverbs

An adverb is a word that describes the verb. It tells how the action takes place. As you are reading, record verb and adverb pairs (e.g., he

---

Adjectives and Adverbs

How many interesting **adjectives** (describing words) can you find as you are reading?

Word Choice

Find a very descriptive passage of the book. Which words are the most effective in helping to create the imagery in your mind?

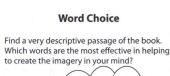

New to Me

Choose three new words. Write each definition and draw a picture to show the meaning.

context of the book. Many words have multiple meanings, and young readers need to become savvy at using the dictionary and the context cues of the text to determine the way in which words are being used.

GUESS AND CHECK

As readers, we use a number of contextual clues to determine the meaning of new words. In this task box, young readers record five words that are new to them and guess the meaning of the word. They then use a dictionary to verify and record the definition. As in the New to Me task, ensure that students have selected the appropriate meaning for the words they have selected.

SYNONYMS AND ANTONYMS

Students select five interesting words from the text and use a thesaurus to find a synonym and antonym for each word. It may not be possible for students to locate the required information for each word; encourage students to use a dictionary and record the definition of the word instead.

USING THE DICTIONARY AND THESAURUS

This task helps students become familiar with the resources available to interpret the English language. Readers select four interesting words; they use a dictionary to locate the definition and a thesaurus to identify a synonym. Some dictionaries are quite intimidating for young readers, as the definitions can seem to complicate rather than clarify understanding of a word. Consider a mini-lesson to assist students in deciphering which parts of a dictionary definition are helpful in determining word meaning.

INSTEAD OF "SAID"

How many different ways can you say the same thing? This task challenges students to find as many different ways of saying "said" as possible. Using the text, readers identify a number of different ways of referring to speech. Later, students can refer to this task to support and enrich their personal writing.

WORD USE

Understanding the meaning of new vocabulary is only a part of language acquisition. In order to integrate new vocabulary into learning, students must also understand appropriate ways they can use these words. In this activity, students identify three new and interesting words, record their definitions and pronunciations, and use each in a sentence.

GLOSSARY

A glossary is usually a text feature in a non-fiction text. Students are challenged to create a glossary for the book they are reading by selecting six new and interesting words. Some students may record the words and organize them in alphabetical order before writing the word meaning beside each word. Some students might use a dictionary to determine the definition of the words; others might use the context cues in the text to construct their own meaning for the words.

Guess and Check

Use the Guess and Check chart below to show how you found the meaning of new words.

Synonyms and Antonyms

Choose five interesting words from the book. Use a thesaurus to find a synonym and an antonym for each word.

Using the Dictonary and Thesaurus

Choose three words from the story to complete the following chart. These should be words that you feel demonstrate the author's word choice.

Instead of "Said"

How many interesting words can you find that the author used to replace the word "said"?

Word Use

Find three interesting words that are new to you. Use a dictionary to help you find their meanings and pronunciation. Use each word in a sentence.

Glossary

Create a **glossary** for new vocabulary you've learned while reading.

_____ _____

_____

Three Words and Pictures

Record three interesting words from the book. Draw a picture to show what they mean.

Word: _____

Word: _____

Word: _____

Six Words and Pictures

Write some new words that you learned while reading. Draw a picture to show what they mean.

Word Collector

Become a **word collector** of interesting and unique words. How many words can you have in your word sack?

Alphabetical Order

Record five interesting words from the book.

1. _____
2. _____
3. _____
4. _____
5. _____

Now reorganize the words so that they are in alphabetical order.

1. _____
2. _____
3. _____
4. _____
5. _____

Word Search

Create a word search about the story using character names, place names, and new vocabulary you have learned. Share it with a friend.

Word List

Initial Sound

Find pairs of words that have the same beginning sound (for example, **br**ight and **br**own)

Adjectives

How many adjectives (describing words) can you find? For example: *big brown* bear

adjectives

Verbs in Action

Verbs are action words *(run, twist, fly* and *crawl)*. Write some verbs from your book and illustrate the action they represent.

Nouns

A **noun** is a person, place, or thing. How many different kinds of nouns can you find in the book?

People	Places	Things

Adjectives, Verbs, and Nouns

Pick one page in the book. How many adjectives, nouns, and verbs can you find on this one page? Write them below:

Adjectives

Verbs

Nouns

Adverbs

An adverb is a word that describes the verb. It tells how the action takes place. As you are reading, record verb and adverb pairs (e.g., he *jogged swiftly* through the forest).

⬆ Verb   ⬆ Adverb

Verb:	Adverb:	Verb:	Adverb:
Verb:	Adverb:	Verb:	Adverb:
Verb:	Adverb:	Verb:	Adverb:
Verb:	Adverb:	Verb:	Adverb:

Adjectives and Adverbs

How many interesting **adjectives** (describing words) can you find as you are reading?

How many interesting **adverbs** can you find? Adverbs are words that describe how the action (verb) happened. Hint: most adverbs end in – *ly*.

Word Choice

Find a very descriptive passage of the book. Which words are the most effective in helping to create the imagery in your mind?

New to Me

Choose three new words. Write each definition and draw a picture to show the meaning.

Word	Definition	Picture

Guess and Check

Use the Guess and Check chart below to show how you found the meaning of new words.

Unknown word	Clues (clues in the text to help determine its meaning)	Guess (what I think it means)	Check (what the dictionary says the word means)

Synonyms and Antonyms

Choose five interesting words from the book. Use a thesaurus to find a synonym and an antonym for each word.

Word	Synonym	Antonym

Using the Dictionary and Thesaurus

Choose three words from the story to complete the following chart. These should be words that you feel demonstrate the author's word choice.

Words	Use a dictionary to find the definition	Use a thesaurus to find a synonym

Instead of "Said"

How many interesting words can you find that the author used to replace the word "said"?

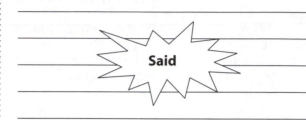

Said

Word Use

Find three interesting words that are new to you. Use a dictionary to help you find their meanings and pronunciation. Use each word in a sentence.

Word:_____ Pronunciation:_____
Definition:_____
Sentence: _____
_____

Word:_____ Pronunciation:_____
Definition:_____
Sentence: _____
_____

Word:_____ Pronunciation:_____
Definition:_____
Sentence: _____
_____

Glossary

Create a *glossary* for new vocabulary you've learned while reading.

Rubric for Word Skills

Skill	Level 1	Level 2	Level 3	Level 4
Identify and demonstrate an understanding of new vocabulary	Student demonstrates a limited understanding of new vocabulary.	Student demonstrates a satisfactory understanding of new vocabulary.	Student demonstrates a good understanding of new vocabulary.	Student demonstrates an excellent understanding of new vocabulary.
Identify and record examples of various parts of speech (nouns, verbs, adjectives, adverbs)	Student is rarely able to identify, describe, and provide examples of the various parts of speech.	Student is able to identify, describe, and provide examples of some of the various parts of speech.	Student is able to identify, describe, and provide examples of the various parts of speech.	Student is consistently able to identify, describe, and provide examples of the various parts of speech.
Use a variety of strategies to decode new vocabulary	Student uses few strategies to decode and understand new vocabulary.	Student uses some strategies to decode and understand new vocabulary.	Student uses many strategies to decode and understand new vocabulary.	Student effectively uses a variety of strategies to decode and understand new vocabulary.
Use a dictionary and thesaurus to strengthen understanding of words	Student finds it challenging to use a dictionary and thesaurus to strengthen his/her understanding of new words.	Student sometimes uses a dictionary and thesaurus with some accuracy to strengthen his/her understanding of new words.	Student uses a dictionary and thesaurus to strengthen his/her understanding of new words.	Student proficiently uses a dictionary and thesaurus to strengthen his/her understanding of new words.

5 Box 4: Taxonomy of Thinking

Many years ago, Dr. Benjamin Bloom proposed a multi-level approach to learning. He suggested that, as learners, we begin with very concrete levels of thinking and move toward deeper understanding. More recently a former student of Benjamin Bloom, Lorin Anderson and a group of psychologists revisited Bloom's taxonomy and presented a revised version (2001) thought to be more relevant in the 21st century. As a result, there were a number of changes that were made to the original taxonomy proposed by Bloom.

Bloom's Taxonomy Revised

1. Remembering
2. Understanding
3. Applying
4. Analyzing
5. Evaluating
6. Creating

1. The first level of thinking is referred to as Remembering. At this level we are able to recall information that we have encountered, but have little need to change it, use it, or understand it. We simply *know* it.

2. The second level is Understanding. At this level we grasp information and are able to compare or contrast ideas, and even retell using our own words. We are able to *explain* it.

3. Moving beyond comprehension, we learn to use the information that we have learned. This level is called Application. At this level, learners are able to demonstrate knowledge, solve problems, or apply what they know to new and similar situations. We *use* it.

4. Once we can apply something, we can begin to analyze this information. At the Analysis level, we can classify or categorize information. We are able to deconstruct something that we have learned into separate elements in order to think about the parts and how they fit together. We *examine* it.

5. At the Evaluation level, we are able to make choices and judgments about information. We see the value of the new learning and identify ways in which it is beneficial. We *assess* it.

6. Finally, the highest level of thinking is the level at which we are able to use the information we have learned to create something new. At the Creating level of thinking, we are able to combine new learning with our existing knowledge and synthesize it into something unique. We *integrate* it.

More recently, this familiar taxonomy has been simplified even further by grouping some of the levels of the taxonomy together.

- Tony Stead (2004) describes the early levels of thinking (Remembering and Understanding) as *literal understanding* of text. In these levels, readers are using the text as the foundation for all understanding and comprehension. All meaning is generated by the text. Tasks that monitor student's literal understanding require students to be able to read text, understand it, and recall facts.

- The middle two levels of thinking (Application and Analysis) both address the reader's ability to form an *interpretative understanding* of text. This level of thinking requires students to construct meaning that is beyond the stated facts in the text. The text provides the basic understanding and the reader brings meaning to the text.
- Finally, *evaluative understanding* includes the higher levels of thinking (Evaluation and Creating). At this level of understanding, readers use implicit and explicit information from the text to create meaning. Readers must combine personal experiences with the text to construct a personal interpretation of the text.

Overview of Bloom's Taxonomy

Types of Understanding (Stead 2004)		Bloom's Taxonomy	Behavior Descriptions	Connections to Reading
Literal Understanding		Remembering	Recall of something but without having to change it, use it, or understand it. Knowing the facts.	Recall information from the text.
		Understanding	Explaining new learning; ability to compare, contrast, or retell.	Demonstrate an understanding of the text.
Interpretive Understanding		Applying	Use of new learning to solve situations or new problems in an appropriate ways.	Apply information from the text to new situations
		Analyzing	Taking apart something learned into separate elements, and thinking about the parts and how they fit together.	Demonstrate an understanding of the various components of the text.
Evaluative Understanding		Evaluating	Forming judgments about information or new learning,	Make judgments based on information from the text.
		Creating	Generating or creating something new by combining or connecting ideas in a new way.	Combine information from the text in new and creative ways.

Increasingly Complex

Connecting Bloom's Taxonomy to Reading Skills

As students become stronger readers and are presented with increasingly challenging books, they fluctuate between levels with which they are able to think about the text. Rather than seeing reading as a linear progression through Bloom's Taxonomy, students jump between the various levels of thinking, depending on their understanding of the text. If a student is spending a great deal of time trying to decode new words and formulate an understanding of the concepts in the text, he or she is not likely to be able to use the higher levels of thinking. However, the same student, when presented with a different text, may feel quite comfortable evaluating the information and using it creatively.

Consider for a moment two different texts that you are able to read. You are familiar with all of the vocabulary and have a genuine interest in the subject matter. Let's think of one as a novel that you have been reading for enjoyment, and the other the installation manual for your new dishwasher. Beginning with your novel you are probably quite comfortable with the higher-order levels of thinking. I'm sure you could think critically about the content, analyze the facts presented and compare them with your existing knowledge on the subject matter. With ease you could evaluate the actions of a character and consider how you may have acted differently. Now consider the other text: the dishwasher manual. How comfortable with higher-order thinking would you be with this text? Pretend that you are able to read and understand the instructions—although even this may be a stretch for some of us. Now pretend that you've opened your kitchen cabinet and discovered that your pipes are not exactly where the instruction manual promised they would be. Now how are your application skills? Can you figure out where to attach the pipes? Let's now pretend that you do not even see pipes when you opened your cupboard. Could you figure out the purpose of each pipe and wire, find their origin, and formulate new ways to attach them to your new dishwasher? Can you analyze the components that make your dishwasher function? For the true higher-order thinkers: can you use your new found knowledge creatively by combining your understanding of plumbing and electricity with the information in your manual to safely and successfully install your dishwasher? Finally, what about evaluation? Have you concluded by now that the manual is useless and the only text that you need to be able to read effectively is the phone directory to find the number of the nearest plumber?

The relationship between level of thinking and level of text is an inverse one: i.e., as the texts increases in difficulty, the student is able to process it at a lower level of thinking, whereas a student has greater success applying higher-order thinking skills to an easier text.

The Key Ideas task is on a non-fiction article "People More Dangerous than Sharks" in *Science in the News* by Jane Sellman; the Character Identification task is on the novel *A Wrinkle in Time* by Madeleine L'Engle.

Remembering
Key Ideas

Can you recall and describe three key ideas from the text?

1. Basking and whale sharks only eat plankton, tiny sea animals and plants.

2. Sharks are disappearing from our planet.

3. Sharks are important for the environment.

Remembering
Character Identification

Identify and describe as many characters as possible.

1. Meg - poor student, stuburn, always crying.
2. Calvin - tall, skinney, red hair, lots of freckles, oldest of the children.
3. Charles Wallace - 3 years old, 1 year away from starting school, very smart, Meg's little brother.
4. Mrs. Whatsit - Very cherry not from Earth.
5. Mrs. Who - Has trouble speaking, friends with Mrs. Whatsit and Which
6. Mrs. Which - Has trouble speaking, leader of the group.

We need to ensure that we are providing opportunities for students to practice the higher levels of thinking. They need to learn how to analyze and evaluate information found in their books and think creatively about the content; however, this is possible only when students are reading a text at a level that is suitable for them. As students choose texts of increasing difficulty, they may lose some ground with their ability to think deeply about it. By providing regular opportunities for students to practice these various levels of thinking, they will find ways of adapting them to a greater variety of texts.

The task boxes that address the earlier levels of understanding (Remembering and Understanding, page 55) require students to think about the literal interpretation of the text. These tasks target their comprehension of the basic content of the book. They can be completed with information that is found in the text, and the student is required to do very little interpretation of the text.

Analyzing tasks provide an opportunity for students to connect their own thinking with the information found in the text. Students complete these tasks using their own thinking as well as information found in their books. They must have a good understanding of the text in order to think critically of it.

The Fiction or Non-Fiction? task is on *Anastasia's Album* by Hugh Brewster; the Who's Most Important? task is on the novel *Barely Hanging On* by Karen Rivers.

Analyzing
Fiction or Non-Fiction?
How do you know that this text is fiction or non-fiction? Give as many reasons as you can.

I know this text is non-fiction because on the spine of the book it has a Dewey decimal. I also know because it is facts and photos written in the book. I also know because they have quotes from her tutors and samples of letters and sections of the Tsars diary. Finally, it has sequences like "the war years".

Analyzing
Who's Most Important?
Which character do you think is the most important to the plot? Why?

I think Carly is the most important character in the book because she is telling the story, everything in the book is about her life. Another thing is that if there was no Carly there would be no story and if Carly got re-placed then the story would be all wrong.

The Evaluating task is on the book *Secret Santa* by Sabrina James; the "Dear Diary" task box is a Creating task on *Goldilocks and the Three Bears*, retold by Jan Brett.

Evaluating
Do you agree with the decisions made by the main character? Would you have acted differently? Explain your thinking.

No, I do not agree with the main character's decisions in the book. When she was trying to find out who was her secret santa I would have watched people. I know. Not like what she had did. The main character in my book assumed it was the boy she liked.

(She was wrong)

"Dear Diary"
Write a diary entry that one of the characters may have written before, during or after one of the book's events.

Dear Diary,
I was sad because Goldilocks used all of my stuff. I was so hungry and there was no food for me. She broke my favourite chair. I hope Papa Bear fixes my chair.

Evaluating and Creating tasks allow students to judge and evaluate the information found in the text. When evaluating, students are encouraged to think critically about the text and assess it. When creating, students are connecting information from the text with things they already know to create something new and different.

Literal Understanding Task Descriptions

The task boxes that address the first levels of Bloom's Taxonomy rely on students' Literal Understanding of text. These include tasks that target students' remembering and understanding of the text. Tasks that strengthen student's Interpretative Understanding of the text ask students to apply and analyze the information from the text. Finally, when evaluating and creating from the text, students are thinking on an Evaluative Understanding level about the text.

REMEMBERING: WHAT'S HAPPENING?

In this task, students recall the most exciting part of the story. They are invited to include a picture to support their ideas. This activity relies on students remembering critical information from the text and being able to retell it using their own words.

REMEMBERING: CHARACTER IDENTIFICATION

Recalling and describing characters demands that readers have a good knowledge of the text. They may need to revisit the text to find supporting evidence for their ideas or specific details they may wish to include. Some readers may include a great number of characters (including those with minor roles), while others may select fewer characters but provide greater detail when describing them.

REMEMBERING: THREE MAIN IDEAS

In this task, students recall and summarize three key ideas from the text. When reading fiction, students may choose to describe various elements of the text, such as setting, characters, or plot. They may retell these ideas with great detail and supporting evidence, or they may briefly summarize the information with little attention to details. When reading non-fiction, readers may describe three important facts from the text. Again, some readers may be quite brief, while others may include supporting details for each of the three key ideas they describe.

REMEMBERING: THE 5 W'S

The five W's are the *who, what, when, where,* and *why* of any given story. In this task, readers think about the 5 W's in relation to the text they are reading: Who is the story about? What happens in the story? When does the story take place? Where does the story take place? And why is there a problem? This comprehensive approach to remembering the text encourages readers to examine a number of important elements in the text. Through this activity, students will think about the characters, setting, and plot of the story. Encourage students to include as much detail as possible and supporting evidence when available.

The reproducible boxes on pages 60–63 and 66–68 can be copied and placed into Reading 8-Boxes for students' use.

**Remembering
What's Happening?**

Describe the most exciting part of the story. Use a picture to help explain your thinking.

**Remembering
Character Identification**

Identify and describe as many characters as possible.

**Remembering
Three Main Ideas**

Identify three main ideas that are explained in the text.

1. _____

Remembering: The 5 W's

Answer the five W's for the story: Who? What? Where? When? Why?

WHO is the story about?

**Understanding
What's the Problem?**

What is the problem in the story?

_____

**Understanding
Summarizing Important Parts**

In your own words retell the most important part of the story.

**Understanding:
Character Comparison**

Compare and contrast two of the characters in the story.

**Understanding
Three Main Ideas**

Describe three main ideas that are explained in the text. Tell why each is important.

1. _____

**Applying
Lessons to Learn**

What do you think is the most important thing that you learned from the story? Tell why.

**Applying
What's Most Important?**

What do you think is the most important thing to remember from this book?

UNDERSTANDING: WHAT'S THE PROBLEM?

Students think about the problem in the story and explain the ways in which the problem is solved. Students will demonstrate their understanding of the various components of the plot as they describe the conflict and resolution of the story. Some students may provide great detail, including supporting evidence from the text; others may give a very rudimentary description of the plot elements.

UNDERSTANDING: SUMMARIZING IMPORTANT PARTS

When summarizing, students are thinking about the most important parts of the story and using their own words to express their thinking in concise ways. A summary should be brief and clear. Effective summaries will have a clear focus and provide just enough information to demonstrate a good understanding of the text.

UNDERSTANDING: CHARACTER COMPARISON

In this task, readers compare and contrast two characters from the story. Students need to find ways in which the characters are similar and ways in which they differ. Some students may provide responses based on the obvious features and characteristics of the characters (appearance, age, description, etc), whereas others may form deeper connections between the characters, such as personality, motivation, morality, background and experiences, etc.

UNDERSTANDING: THREE MAIN IDEAS

Summarizing main ideas requires students to identify and demonstrate an understanding of the concepts that the author considers important in the text. In this task box, students identify three main ideas and describe each briefly. When conferencing with students, it is interesting to observe their rationale for selecting the ideas they choose to describe. Some may be able to articulate clearly their selections, drawing attention to text features and supporting evidence, while other students may find it harder to explain their choices.

Interpretative Understanding Task Descriptions

APPLYING: LESSONS TO LEARN

This task requires readers to think about the important lessons they may have learned while reading the text. Some students may be able to form complex inferences, identifying overall themes and moral implications that may be present throughout the entire text. Other students may have a more limited understanding of the text as a whole and refer to specific instances in which important lessons were demonstrated.

APPLYING: WHAT'S MOST IMPORTANT?

This task asks student to describe the important things to remember from the book and justify their thinking. Some students may refer directly to facts or main ideas that are either directly stated or implicitly present throughout the book; others may describe the overall tone or theme of the book; and others may refer to a specific element in the text that aided in their understanding of the book as a whole. With non-fiction, readers may describe interesting new learning that took place and describe ways in which this learning may be applied in the future.

Applying
Plan of Action

Use the clues in the story to develop a plan of action for one of the characters. Based on what you know, what advice could you give this character?

Analyzing
Fiction Facts

Make a list of the events in the story that indicate that it is fiction.

○ _____

_____

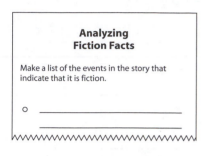

Analyzing
Fiction or Non-Fiction

How do you know that this text is fiction or non-fiction? Give as many reasons as you can.

Analyzing
Ordering Important Events

List the three most important events in the story. Put them in order of the most important or exciting event to the least important or exciting.

Analyzing
Who's Most Important?

Which character do you think is the most important to the plot? Why?

_____

_____

Analyzing
PMI Chart

Record four facts from the text. For each fact, think about Plus (positive), Minus (negative), and Interesting ideas you have about it.

Fact	Plus	Minus	Interesting

APPLYING: PLAN OF ACTION

As active readers, we are constantly thinking ahead and formulating predictions based on our prior knowledge and experiences, and information from the text. This activity has readers create a plan of action for one of the characters, providing advice he/she may follow in order to resolve some element of conflict in the story. The varied backgrounds of students will play a large role in the wide range of possible responses for this task.

ANALYZING: FICTION FACTS

Critical readers need to be able to decipher the subtle differences between fiction and reality. This task invites readers to carefully examine specific events in the story that indicate that the text is fiction. Readers must be able to use a variety of prior experiences and personal connections in order to accurately identify fictional components. Some genres of text, such as realistic fiction, may be more challenging than others, so readers may need to think not only about the content of the story, but about the text elements and features as well. In the case of realistic fiction, a prologue or epilogue may provide readers with some insight into the fictional components of the text.

ANALYZING: FICTION OR NON-FICTION

As in the previous task, readers review the various text features as well as the content of the book to provide evidence whether the text is fiction or non-fiction. A reader who has had a wide range of experiences with a number of different genres of books might find this task easier than students with more limited text experiences.

ANALYZING: ORDERING IMPORTANT EVENTS

In this task, readers select the three most important or exciting events in the story and rank them in order from most exciting to least exciting. By summarizing the events, students are demonstrating their general understanding of the text; however, by ranking them and justifying their thinking, students are able to think more critically about the text. When conferencing with students, ask them to share their rationale for their choices, not only their selection of events as most interesting/exciting, but also their reasons for placing events in the order that they did.

ANALYZING: WHO'S MOST IMPORTANT?

Most plots are dependent on the interaction of a number of characters. In this task, readers analyze the roles played by the various characters and indicate which character they think is the most important to the plot. Initially, it may seem that the main character is the obvious choice; however, some more critical readers may consider the role of the villain or even minor characters as they lead up to the conflict in the story.

ANALYZING: PMI CHART

This PMI chart asks students to record the Plus (positive), Minus (negative), and Interesting things about four facts from the book. As students think about the implications about the facts presented in the text, they are actively analyzing the facts in the text and thinking critically about it using their prior knowledge, experiences, and opinions.

Remembering
What's Happening?

Describe the most exciting part of the story. Use a picture to help explain your thinking.

_____

_____

_____

_____

Remembering
Character Identification

Identify and describe as many characters as possible.

_____

_____

_____

_____

_____

_____

_____

_____

_____

_____

Remembering
Three Main Ideas

Identify three main ideas that are explained in the text.

1. _____

_____

_____

2. _____

_____

_____

3. _____

_____

_____

Remembering: The 5 W's

Answer the five W's for the story: Who? What? Where? When? Why?

WHO is the story about?

WHAT happens in the story?

WHEN does the story take place?

WHERE does the story take place?

WHY is there a problem?

Understanding
What's the Problem?

What is the problem in the story?

_____

_____

_____

_____

Explain how the problem is solved.

_____

_____

_____

_____

Understanding
Summarizing Important Parts

In your own words retell the most important part of the story.

_____

_____

_____

_____

_____

_____

_____

_____

_____

Understanding
Character Comparison

Compare and contrast two of the characters in the story.

_____

_____

_____

_____

_____

_____

_____

_____

Understanding
Three Main Ideas

Describe three main ideas that are explained in the text. Tell why each is important.

1. _____

_____

_____

2. _____

_____

_____

3. _____

_____

_____

Applying
Lessons to Learn

What do you think is the most important thing that you learned from the story? Tell why.

_____

_____

_____

_____

_____

_____

_____

_____

Applying
What's Most Important?

What do you think is the most important thing to remember from this book?

_____

_____

_____

_____

Why do you think it is important?

_____

_____

_____

_____

_____

Applying
Plan of Action

Use the clues in the story to develop a plan of action for one of the characters. Based on what you know, what advice could you give this character?

_____

_____

_____

_____

_____

_____

_____

Analyzing
Fiction Facts

Make a list of the events in the story that indicate that it is fiction.

○ _____

_____

○ _____

_____

○ _____

_____

○ _____

_____

Analyzing
Fiction or Non-Fiction

How do you know that this text is fiction or non-fiction? Give as many reasons as you can.

_____

_____

_____

_____

_____

_____

_____

_____

Analyzing
Ordering Important Events

List the three most important events in the story. Put them in order of the most important or exciting event to the least important or exciting.

Most important/exciting event:

_____

_____

Second most important/exciting:

_____

_____

Least most important/exciting event:

_____

_____

Analyzing
Who's Most Important?

Which character do you think is the most important to the plot? Why?

_____

_____

_____

_____

_____

_____

_____

Analyzing
PMI Chart

Record four facts from the text. For each fact, think about Plus (positive), Minus (negative), and Interesting ideas you have about it.

Fact	Plus	Minus	Interesting

Evaluative Understanding Task Descriptions

**Evaluating
Interesting Facts**

Write three facts from the text and tell why
each was important or interesting.

Fact #1: _____

**Evaluating
Favorite Part**

What was your favorite part?

_____

_____

**Evaluating
Fairness**

Do you think the main character was treated
fairly? Explain your thinking.

_____

**Evaluating
"I Disagree"**

Describe one time when you disagreed with
the actions of one of the characters.

_____

_____

**Evaluating
Admirable Character Traits**

What are some of the traits that you admire
about the main character of the story?

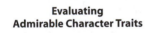

**Evaluating
Interesting Facts**

Write three facts from the text and tell why
each was important or interesting.

Fact #1: _____

EVALUATING: INTERESTING PART

This task box for younger readers provides them with the opportunity to identify a part of the book that they found most interesting and justify their choice. By justifying their selection, students are judging the importance and relevance of the event.

EVALUATING: FAVORITE PART

Selecting a favorite part invites students to describe personal connections they may have made to the text while reading. Even when reading the same book, different students could select a wide range of favorite parts, according to previous experiences they bring to the text. The most important part of this task is providing students with the opportunity to justify their selection.

EVALUATING: FAIRNESS

Reflecting on the actions of all characters and the ways in which they are treated encourages readers to evaluate the author's intent. In this task, students think about the way the main character is treated and decide if it is fair. Examining the elements of fairness throughout the book, students will have an opportunity to consider the various actions of the characters and the outcomes that result.

EVALUATING: "I DISAGREE!"

When readers are given the opportunity to state their approval or disapproval of a character's actions, they are forming an evaluative conclusion. As part of an ongoing dialogue between the reader and the text, we continually evaluate the decisions of the author and the actions and words of the various characters. This task invites students to describe one time when they may have disagreed with the actions of one of the characters, and explain ways in which the reader thinks the character should have acted.

EVALUATING: ADMIRABLE CHARACTER TRAITS

As readers become more familiar with characters in the text, they recognize and connect with their various traits. In this task, students select one character from the text and describe the traits that they admire most in them. More sophisticated readers will think of traits that describe the character's moral perspective or defining beliefs, rather than the obvious physical or outward appearances. The graphic organizer provided in this task encourages students to be creative with their responses.

EVALUATING: INTERESTING FACTS

This task invites readers to select three facts from the text. For each fact, students retell the fact, and then describe why they thought the fact was interesting or especially relevant. As they evaluate the importance of the different facts, students may form connections to their personal experiences or to other selections of the same text.

**Creating
Plot Changes**

How could you change the plot to make it appeal to a different audience?

CREATING: PLOT CHANGES

In this task, readers consider alterations they could make to the plot for it to appeal to a different audience. The reader must consider an alternative audience and think about appropriate changes that would make the book seem more inviting to that specific group.

**Creating
Alternative Solution**

Can you think of an original way for the characters to solve their problem?

CREATING: ALTERNATIVE SOLUTION

This activity enables readers to think about the climax of the plot and about alternative resolutions. Some students may consider some of the implications that one significant change may have brought about to the story. As students combine the text with their own thinking, they are synthesizing the information in new and creative ways.

**Creating
New Summary**

Create the summary to put at the back of the book. It needs to tell what the book is about without giving too much away. What would

CREATING: NEW SUMMARY

The information on the back cover of a book usually provides prospective readers with just enough information to have a general idea of what the book will be about, without giving away too much about the content of the text. In this task, readers create an effective summary for the back of the book. They may include a picture and other information to capture the reader's interest.

**Creating
"Dear Diary"**

Write a diary entry that one of the characters may have written before, during, or after one of the book's events.

Dear Diary:

_____

CREATING: "DEAR DIARY"

Why not just jump into the story in role as one of the characters? In this task, readers write a diary entry in role as one of the characters. They should choose a significant event in the text and write an entry before, during, or after it happens. Writing in role will allow students to think about the numerous factors that may have influenced the characters while making decisions throughout the event. Students can think about the characters' emotions, actions, surroundings, circumstances, and countless other factors.

**Creating
Who's Like You?**

Which character can you relate to the most? Give examples from the book and your life to show how you are similar.

CREATING: WHO'S LIKE YOU?

As readers, we often feel empathy for characters that we relate to. In this task, students select one character from the book and describe ways in which that character is similar to themselves. Using personal experiences to connect to characters enables the reader to form stronger bonds with them and have a deep insight into their thoughts, actions, and decisions. It also causes greater internal conflict when a much-loved character reacts in a way that the reader may disagree with.

**Creating
Alternative Actions**

Do you agree with the decisions made by the main character? Would you have acted differently? Explain your thinking.

CREATING: ALTERNATIVE ACTIONS

In this task box, students are asked whether or not they agree with the decisions made by the main character. Readers think about the ways they may have reacted had they been in the position of the main character. Readers continually evaluate and judge the decisions made by the author. Examining the character's motivation or actions from a critical perspective enables students to consider a situation from a different point of view.

Evaluating
Interesting Part

Draw and write about the part of the book that you found the most interesting. Tell why you selected this part.

_____

_____

_____

Evaluating
Favorite Part

What was your favorite part?

_____

_____

_____

_____

Why?

_____

_____

_____

_____

Evaluating
Fairness

Do you think the main character was treated fairly? Explain your thinking.

_____

_____

_____

_____

_____

_____

_____

Evaluating
"I Disagree"

Describe one time when you disagreed with the actions of one of the characters.

_____

_____

_____

_____

How do you think he/she should have acted?

_____

_____

_____

Evaluating
Admirable Character Traits

What are some of the traits that you admire about the main character of the story?

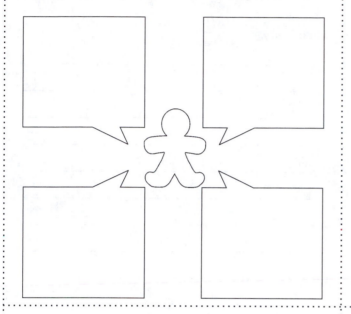

Evaluating
Interesting Facts

Write three facts from the text and tell why each was important or interesting.

Fact #1: _____

_____

It's interesting because:

_____

_____

Fact #2: _____

It's interesting because:

_____

_____

Fact #3: _____

It's interesting because:

_____

Creating
Plot Changes

How could you change the plot to make it appeal to a different audience?

_____

_____

_____

_____

_____

_____

_____

_____

_____

Creating
Alternative Solution

Can you think of an original way for the characters to solve their problem?

_____

_____

_____

_____

_____

_____

_____

_____

Creating
New Summary

Create the summary to put at the back of the book. It needs to tell what the book is about without giving too much away. What would you say? What picture would you include to capture your reader's interest?

_____

_____

_____

_____

_____

_____

Creating
"Dear Diary"

Write a diary entry that one of the characters may have written before, during, or after one of the book's events.

Dear Diary,

_____

_____

_____

_____

_____

_____

_____

_____

_____

Creating
Who's Like You?

Which character can you relate to the most? Give examples from the book and your life to show how you are similar.

_____

_____

_____

_____

_____

_____

_____

_____

Creating
Alternative Actions

Do you agree with the decisions made by the main character? Would you have acted differently? Explain your thinking.

_____

_____

_____

_____

_____

_____

_____

_____

Rubric for Taxonomy

	Skill	Level 1	Level 2	Level 3	Level 4
Literal Understanding	**Remembering** Recall information from the text	Little information from the text is recalled accurately.	Some information from the text is recalled accurately.	Most information from the text is recalled accurately.	All relevant information from the text is recalled and presented clearly.
	Understanding Demonstrate an understanding of the text	Demonstrates limited understanding of the content of the text.	Demonstrates some understanding of the content of the text.	Demonstrates a good understanding of the content of the text.	Demonstrates a thorough understanding of the content of the text.
Interpretative Understanding	**Applying** Apply information from the text to new situations	Student is beginning to apply information from the text to new situations.	Student sometimes applies information from the text to new situations.	Student effectively applies information from the text to new situations.	Student effectively applies information from the text to new situations in innovative and creative ways.
	Analyzing Demonstrate an understanding of the various components of the text	Student finds it challenging to describe the various elements and components of the text.	Student is sometimes able to describe the various elements and components of the text.	Student is able to describe the various elements and components of the text.	Student is able to describe the various elements and components of the text, and to describe the ways in which they fit together to form a unified text.
Evaluative Understanding	**Evaluating** Make judgments based on information from the text	Student is rarely able to make judgments based on information from the text.	Student is beginning to make judgments based on information from the text.	Student is able to make judgments based on information from the text.	Student is able to make judgments based on information from the text, and to support his/her thinking with evidence from the book and his/her own thinking.
	Creating Combine information from the text in new and creative ways	Student rarely combines information from the text with his/her own ideas.	Student sometimes combines information from the text with his/her own ideas.	Student can creatively combine information from the text with his/her own ideas.	Student can creatively combine information from the text with his/her own ideas, resulting in original ways of thinking of the text.

6 Boxes 5–8: Reading Strategies

Metacognition is the ability to think about our thinking. As we help students understand the strategies used by effective readers, providing strong instruction on comprehension strategies and time for guided practice, students will become more metacognitively aware.

Metacognition has rapidly become an essential skill for students and an important area of reading instruction for teachers. The reading strategies—connecting, inferring, questioning, visualizing, determining importance, and synthesizing—introduced by Harvey and Goudvis (2000 and 2007) have formed the foundation for effective reading instruction. Many of the tasks that make up a Reading 8-Box are designed as tools to strengthen students understanding and application of these reading strategies.

Each Reading 8-Box should contain four tasks that target different reading comprehension strategies. Through the regular reinforcement and application of these strategies, students become not only proficient readers, but effective thinkers. They are able to articulate their thinking using correct terminology, integrate the different strategies, and apply them to a variety of texts. As students mature, they need to think about their reading and their thinking, articulate their thinking, and provide evidence from the text to support their ideas. The following task boxes provide many opportunities for students to develop and strengthen these skills.

Monitoring Understanding

Students should stop, think, and react to what they read.

Students need to be aware of their inner conversations as they are reading. The reader should stop frequently, think about the information, and record their thoughts and reactions. In this way they are monitoring their understanding of the text.

Students who are engaged in the active process of reading are continuously checking their understanding of the text. They are aware of the words they are reading, conscious of the meaning of the text, constructing images in their mind, making sense of the action of characters, interpreting the voice of the author, engaging in a dialogue with the text through asking questions and seeking answers, determining the critical ideas… all the while asking themselves, "Does this make sense?" Reading is a very complex process, and yet proficient readers seamlessly flow between these and many other skills necessary to comprehend the text they are reading.

Sometimes students become very skilled at mimicking good reading skills. Have you ever had a student read aloud beautifully with fluency and expression, only to discover later that they had no idea what they had read? Perhaps you have done it yourself. Has your mind ever strayed from a passage of text, and you glanced back only to realize that you have no idea what you have just read?

What strategies would you, as a proficient reader employ? Would you return to an earlier paragraph and attempt a second run at the passage that you had glazed over? Would you refocus your attention, aware of the distractions that may have temporarily diverted you? Would you examine an unfamiliar word or two that may have been critical to the meaning of the text? Perhaps you would continue to read, and return later to the passage you had missed in order to add more meaning to it. Or if you're totally frustrated, would you put down the book and return to it later with a clear head… and a hot cup of coffee?

When children are first exposed to books, they recognize the fact that books contain worlds and stories that can be explored through the pages of the text. Very small children will listen, filled with wonder, to a caregiver read a story, and then will retell the story using the pictures as guides. Often toddlers "read" their loved books over and over again, constructing meaning from pictures and retelling the stories to themselves, their toys, and anyone else who is willing to listen. As they grow, we introduce them to the written word. We teach them about letters, phonics, and words. They learn that letters form words, and words form sentences. We teach them to decode, sound out, and recognize words. We introduce them to punctuation and syntax. Suddenly the concept of a book has changed from containing exciting stories and adventures to a puzzle of letters, words, and symbols. Children often become so engrossed with decoding the words that they forget that the most important part of reading is not the words themselves, but the meaning that they convey. We need to ensure that even our youngest readers recognize that reading is so much more than the words on the page. It is important to encourage students to reflect on their reading, question, predict, and connect with the text in addition to decoding the words.

We need to teach students to pause while reading and contemplate the things they have read. We have to teach them to interact and react with the text. Starting from the earliest readers, our students must learn how to self-monitor their understanding. They require strategies to monitor and correct their comprehension of text. These strategies need to be actively taught. As we move students from non-readers to early readers we should never alter the focus from the meaning of the text to the text in isolation. Reading requires generating meaning and thinking about that meaning, not only decoding the words on the pages.

The Using Pictures sample looks at the illustrations of the non-fiction text *All About Canadian Communities: Rural Communities.*

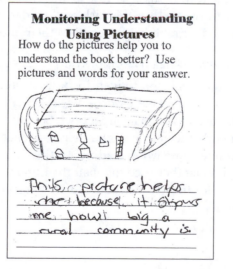

Monitoring Understanding Using Pictures
How do the pictures help you to understand the book better? Use pictures and words for your answer.

This picture helps me because it shows me how big a rural community is.

Monitoring Understanding Using Prompts
How do you check to be sure that you are understanding while you read?
I visualize the exact describing words that I say in my head.

What helps you identify ideas while you are reading?
What characters say in the book helps me make ideas.

What helps you to "read between the lines"?
Clues from the text help me read between the lines.

How do you know if you are not understanding?
I do not know what is going on in the book and I am confused.

What 'fix-up' strategies work effectively for you?
I re-read what I have read.

Tasks that target students' understanding are intended to help readers reflect on the strategies they use to strengthen their comprehension of texts. The Using Pictures task on page 71 is intended for younger readers; students examine the text features (in this case, illustrations of the non-fiction text *All About Canadian Communities: Rural Communities*) and describe ways in which they help to strengthen their understanding of the text. Encouraging younger students to respond with pictures and words will allow them greater versatility to explain their thinking. Some young readers may choose to copy a diagram from the text, then explain how it strengthens their understanding of a particular topic. Likewise, it may be interesting to note students' misconceptions in their understanding of various texts. This provides teachers an opportunity to redirect student learning and ensure that the student is meeting with success throughout their reading.

The Using Prompts task on page 71 is intended for an older student and requires a lot more self-reflection. Students identify and justify strategies that they use to repair their comprehension and make inferences. They are asked to think further and describe how they can identify when they are struggling to understand a text. Finally they need to evaluate their fix-up strategies and determine which ones help them to meet with success. Examining responses to this task could provide a great deal of insight into a student's ability to monitor their comprehension. Perhaps, it may be noted that the student has a broad range of strategies, or perhaps the opposite is true. It may be the case that the student uses a wide range of strategies but is unable to articulate them. Whatever the case, this task provides a deeper insight into a student's understanding of their own metacognition.

Monitoring Understanding Task Descriptions

Below are several thinking boxes that target student's metacognition. Most tasks that assess students understanding are suitable for both fiction and non-fiction.

MONITORING UNDERSTANDING USING PICTURES

Using the pictures/images in the text, students generate a stronger understanding of the text. Images provide mental images for students to connect meaningfully with the text. In this task box, students describe the ways in which they used the pictures to help strengthen their understanding.

MONITORING UNDERSTANDING: STRATEGIES FOR REPAIRING COMPREHENSION

Young readers begin to identify basic strategies for repairing comprehension. They may think of basic word-attack skills, such as sounding out words, or looking for smaller words in larger ones. Some students may generate responses that are intended to repair comprehension, such as rereading a section of text, or asking questions while reading. In this task, students describe three different strategies that they used to repair their understanding of the text. This may form the basis for further instruction based on students responses and their strengths and needs.

The reproducible boxes on pages 74–75 can be copied and placed into Reading 8-Boxes for students' use.

Monitoring Understanding Using Pictures

How do the pictures help you to understand the book better? Use pictures and words for your answer.

Monitoring Understanding Strategies for Repairing Comprehension

If you are reading and you come to something you don't know, what are three things that you could do?

1. _____

   _____

**Monitoring Understanding
Evaluating Text**

This text was:

☐ Too easy to read

☐ Just right to read

**Monitoring Understanding
Word Attack and Comprehension**

When you come to a word or phrase you don't understand, how do you solve it?

**Monitoring Understanding
Using Rereading and Reading-on**

How do you know if you need to reread a section of text?

**Monitoring Understanding
Using a Checklist**

What are some questions you asked yourself to make sure that you understood what you were reading?

**Monitoring Understanding
Favorite Fix-Ups**

Which fix-up strategies are your favorites? Pick three strategies that you used to make sure that you were understanding the book and explain how they helped you.

**Monitoring Understanding
Using Prompts**

How do you check to be sure that you are understanding while you read?

MONITORING UNDERSTANDING: EVALUATING TEXT

In this task, readers assess the difficulty level of the text as too easy, just right, or too hard; then they must explain their thinking. Using this information, you can help students select other texts or reflect on the student's perception of their reading ability. When students select texts at the appropriate level of difficulty, their learning will be maximized.

MONITORING UNDERSTANDING: WORD ATTACK AND COMPREHENSION

This task helps students frame their thinking about their metacognition. Students think about their word-attack skills, their basic understanding of the text, and the strategies they use to repair their comprehension of the material they have read. When we know which strategies students are using successfully, we can expand on this success by introducing new approaches into their repertoire of skills.

MONITORING UNDERSTANDING: USING REREADING AND READING-ON

Reflecting on the strategy of rereading helps students strengthen their understanding of their comprehension skills. They are encouraged to think of alternative strategies if rereading or reading-on does not effectively clarify the meaning of the text. This task provides teachers the opportunity to gain some insight into a student's perceptions of strategies to repair comprehension.

MONITORING UNDERSTANDING: USING A CHECKLIST

In this task, students use a checklist to identify which strategies they used while reading, and describe the ways in which they found them helpful. Providing a variety of options for strategies to monitor and repair understanding allows students to reflect on which strategies they have used effectively and which strategies may need strengthening.

MONITORING UNDERSTANDING: FAVORITE FIX-UPS

Good readers use a number of different strategies to monitor and repair their understanding as they read. This task encourages students to reflect on the various strategies that they have in their "reader's tool kit" and describe which strategies work best for them: activating prior knowledge; asking themselves questions as they read; rereading difficult passages of text; sounding out unfamiliar words and using context cues to determine their meaning; etc.

MONITORING UNDERSTANDING: USING PROMPTS

Providing a framework for students to explain their metacognition aids them in expressing which strategies they used effectively, and in evaluating their use. This task box provides students with five prompts to help record the strategies they use to repair their comprehension during reading.

Monitoring Understanding
Using Pictures

How do the pictures help you to understand the book better? Use pictures and words for your answer.

_____

_____

_____

_____

_____

Monitoring Understanding
Strategies for Repairing Comprehension

If you are reading and you come to something you don't know, what are three things that you could do?

1. _____

_____

_____

2. _____

_____

_____

3. _____

_____

_____

Monitoring Understanding
Evaluating Text

This text was:

☐ Too easy to read

☐ Just right to read

☐ Too hard to read

Why?

_____

_____

_____

_____

_____

Monitoring Understanding
Word Attack and Comprehension

When you come to a word or phrase you don't understand, how do you solve it?

_____

_____

How do you figure out what information is important to remember?

_____

_____

What do you do when you get confused during reading?

_____

_____

Monitoring Understanding Using Rereading and Reading-on

How do you know if you need to reread a section of text?

_____
_____
_____
_____

What else can you do if reading on or rereading does not help to clarify the meaning of a section of text?

_____
_____
_____
_____

Monitoring Understanding Using a Checklist

What are some questions you asked yourself to make sure that you understood what you were reading?

☐ I tried to remember what I knew about the topic.

☐ I asked myself questions as I read.

☐ I tried to remember similar books or experiences.

☐ I tried to decide what was the most important information in the book.

☐ I thought about reasons why things happened.

☐ I pictured what was happening.

How did these strategies help you understand the book?

_____

Monitoring Understanding Favorite Fix-Ups

Which fix-up strategies are your favorites? Pick three strategies that you used to make sure that you were understanding the book and explain how they helped you.

Monitoring Understanding Using Prompts

How do you check to be sure that you are understanding while you read?

What helps you identify ideas while you are reading?

What helps you to "read between the lines"?

How do you know if you are not understanding?

What fix-up strategies work effectively for you?

Rubric for Monitoring Understanding

Skill	Level 1	Level 2	Level 3	Level 4
Use a variety of strategies while reading to strengthen understanding of texts	Few strategies are used while reading; student demonstrates a limited understanding of the text.	Some strategies are used to strengthen understanding while reading; student demonstrates a satisfactory understanding of the text.	Many strategies are used to strengthen understanding while reading; student demonstrates a good understanding of the text.	Many strategies are effectively used to strengthen understanding while reading; student demonstrates a thorough understanding of the text.
Identify strategies used to effectively interpret texts	Student demonstrates a limited understanding of metacognitive strategies and is beginning to use them to interpret texts while reading.	Student demonstrates a satisfactory understanding of metacognitive strategies and somewhat uses them to interpret texts while reading.	Student demonstrates a good understanding of metacognitive strategies and uses them to interpret texts while reading.	Student demonstrates a thorough understanding of metacognitive strategies and consistently uses them to interpret texts while reading.
Evaluate the effectiveness of comprehension strategies	Student finds it challenging to describe the effectiveness of the comprehension strategies they used.	Student is beginning to describe the effectiveness of the comprehension strategies they used.	Student effectively describes the effectiveness of the comprehension strategies they used.	Student effectively describes the effectiveness of the comprehension strategies they used; they are able to use a variety of strategies proficiently in different situations.
Evaluate and explain the difficulty level of a text	Student finds it challenging to accurately evaluate the difficulty level of a text and explain his/her thinking.	Student can sometimes evaluate the difficulty level of a text and is beginning to explain his/her thinking.	Student can evaluate the difficulty level of a text and explain his/her thinking with appropriate reasoning.	Student can evaluate the difficulty level of a text and explain his/her thinking with appropriate reasoning, providing examples from the text and connections to prior reading experiences.

Connecting

Students make connections to their own lives, other texts, or what they know (or think they know) about the world. Background knowledge is the information that we already know or believe about a certain topic. We find it easier and more enjoyable to read a text that we can relate to, and have some prior understanding of the subject matter. Would you pick up a physics book, and be able to read and understand the content? That depends on a number of factors. For some of us, the mere mention of the word "physics" forms beads of sweat on the back of our necks and we begin to have flashbacks to a dimly lit high-school room plastered with formulas, symbols, and definitions of obscure words. Others, however, may wonder at the marvels of quantum mechanics and feel their pulse quicken and pupils dilate with excitement at the thought of cold fusion.

Students likewise bring a wealth of prior knowledge and experiences to any given text. For example, one student I've met will devour any book about flight or aerospace engineering. He can identify every form of commercial and military aircraft, and name and describe the purpose of every portion of an airplane. He can accurately define and describe Bernoulli's Principle, and will read and comprehend words far beyond his grade level and ability, because he is so enthralled with the subject matter. His background knowledge about aircraft far surpasses that of his peers. The books he chooses to read would confuse the average child his age but, because of his extensive knowledge on the subject matter, he is able to have a much deeper understanding of these challenging texts.

There are three main ways in which students form connections to texts:

- Text-to-text connections are formed by readers between two or more texts. For example, they may find similar ideas, themes, characters, settings, etc.
- Text-to-self connections are made when readers are able to connect something from a text to their own personal experiences. For example, they may know a person similar to a story book character, or have been in a situation similar to one in the book. Perhaps they have been to the location where the story is set.
- Text-to-world connections are based on connections made between the text and facts that students know about the world. For example, they may have a good understanding about a specific time in history, relevant scientific facts, or recent news events.

There are countless examples of how students can form each of these types of connections. Forming connections to a text helps students to make the text personally relevant.

Tasks to form connections are some of the more open-ended types of tasks. Students can draw on a wide range of prior knowledge in order to make meaningful connections. The first sample on page 78 asks the student to identify specific facts from a non-fiction text (*Helicopters* by Jeffrey Zuehlke) and to describe ways in which he or she was able to connect with them. Students will be able to link a range of personal experiences as they consider the thoughts that facts from the text brought to mind.

The second sample task allows a student to describe a specific idea from the story (*Measle and the Wrathmonk* by Ian Ogilvy) and explain the personal connection that the reader was able to make. Students are reminded of a wide range

When we help our students activate their prior knowledge it becomes easier for them to understand and connect to their reading.

Connecting

How does what you are reading now compare to what you have already read on this topic?

Reading this reminded me about flight because Helicopters use the four forces to fly, just like planes. Also the Helicopters rotars are very much like a planes engine with out a cover. Helicopters have many Roles like Rescue and transporting Planes Also can do many things like this.

Connecting

Did you form any special connections as you were reading? Describe a part of the book that reminded you of something else (another book, an interesting fact, or a personal connection— perhaps a person you know)

In the story:	Reminds me of:
In my story when Measle didn't get to eat good food when Basil ate gormet foods and doughnuts when Measle ate wrinkly carrots and drank brown water with green and red chunks in it. Plus Measle cant be free to play around in the house when Basil plays with a train set.	The first parts of this book reminded of Harry Potter because Harry lived in a broom closet and didn't eat the same food as the family and only got 1 present on his birthday while Dudley got 63. And when guests came to their house Uncle Vernon made Harry cower in his room.

of things as they read, and their responses give us some insight into their previous experiences and knowledge.

When we connect to fiction, we may think about setting, plot, characters, events, theme, etc.; when we form connections to non-fiction, we are thinking about our prior knowledge and experiences about the subject matter. Dividing Connecting tasks into those for fiction and for non-fiction allows the student to think about specific connections to the various components of each text form.

Connecting Task Descriptions: Fiction

The following task boxes provide students with a range of opportunities to form various connections to their texts. Some tasks require full written responses, which will help to strengthen students' reading–writing connections, and other tasks are quite open-ended, allowing for a variety of responses from students. Stronger readers will often refer to the text and provide evidence for their thinking.

CONNECTING TO PERSONAL EXPERIENCES

Students begin to make simple connections by recording personal connections to the text. In this task, they are encouraged to think of a variety of connections that they may be reminded of from the text.

CONNECTING TO ANOTHER BOOK

With this task, students begin to focus their attention on making text-to-text connections. They are required to think about ways in which this text is similar to another that they may have read. Students may form connections based on contents of the text, the style of the author, or some other information in the text (such as a fact that they may have been encountered in another text).

The reproducible boxes on pages 82–85 can be copied and placed into Reading 8-Boxes for students' use.

Connecting to Personal Experiences

What does this story remind you of in your life?

Connecting to Another Book

How is this book similar to another one that you have read?

_____

_____

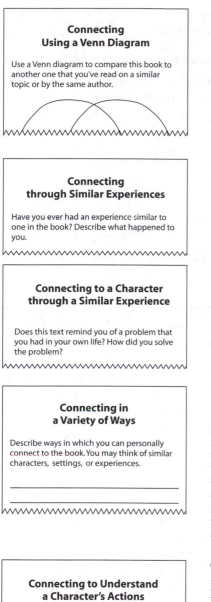

**Connecting to
a Specific Character**

Choose one character in the book who is similar to you. Explain the similarities. (Remember to use examples from the text and your own life.)

**Connecting
Using a Venn Diagram**

Use a Venn diagram to compare this book to another one that you've read on a similar topic or by the same author.

**Connecting
through Similar Experiences**

Have you ever had an experience similar to one in the book? Describe what happened to you.

**Connecting to a Character
through a Similar Experience**

Does this text remind you of a problem that you had in your own life? How did you solve the problem?

**Connecting in
a Variety of Ways**

Describe ways in which you can personally connect to the book. You may think of similar characters, settings, or experiences.

**Connecting to Understand
a Character's Actions**

How does your experience of a similar situation help you to understand the character's actions?

CONNECTING TO A SPECIFIC CHARACTER

Students are invited to make text-to-self connections by examining the ways in which they are similar to or different from one character in the text. They are encouraged to provide evidence in the form of examples from their own life and examples from the text.

CONNECTING USING A VENN DIAGRAM

Students use a graphic organizer (Venn diagram) to record text-to-text connections. They can compare their text to another on a similar topic or by the same author. Students can respond in a variety of ways including using words, phrases, or even images. Some students may include evidence from the text in the form of examples or quotes from the text. When comparing two texts by the same author, students may note similarities in style, word choice, setting, characters, or plot.

CONNECTING THROUGH SIMILAR EXPERIENCES

Empathy is often developed when readers can personally identify with the experiences faced by the characters in the text. This task allows students to express their text-to-self connections as they describe similar experiences that they have faced to the ones encountered in the text.

CONNECTING TO A CHARACTER THROUGH A SIMILAR EXPERIENCE

This task is a natural extension to the previous one. Students examine personal experiences they have faced that are similar to those faced by characters in the text. Readers then evaluate the actions of the characters by comparing their actions to their own.

CONNECTING IN A VARIETY OF WAYS

This open-ended task encourages students to think on their own about personal connections to the text. They are encouraged to think of similar characters, settings, or experiences they may be familiar with. Students may provide a range of personal connections and describe their unique insight into the text that they are reading. Each reader makes different connections to a given text, and it is often interesting to examine the variety of ways that students may connect with their books. Becoming familiar with students' previous experiences and prior knowledge can greatly help us when we are trying to aid students with text selection.

CONNECTING TO UNDERSTAND A CHARACTER'S ACTIONS

Examining the actions of a character based on the reader's previous experiences helps the reader to form stronger text-to-self connections. Often the reader can justify or condemn the actions of a character based on their own personal experiences. Putting themselves "in someone else's shoes" helps readers to understand the dilemmas faced by characters and better understand the choices they make.

Connecting Using a Web

Create a web showing the connections you are able to make while reading. You may choose to put an important image, person, or event in the centre of the web.

Connecting Using a Venn Diagram for a Variety of Connections

Use the Venn diagram to make a text–text, text–self, or text–world connection. Record similarities and differences.

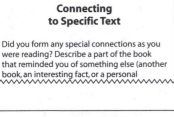

Connecting to Specific Text

Did you form any special connections as you were reading? Describe a part of the book that reminded you of something else (another book, an interesting fact, or a personal

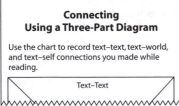

Connecting Using a Three-Part Diagram

Use the chart to record text–text, text–world, and text–self connections you made while reading.

Text–Text

Connecting to Specific Facts

Complete the chart showing connections you made while reading.

Facts I connected with…	These facts made me think of…

Connecting to Previous Reading

How does what you are reading now compare to what you have already read on this topic?

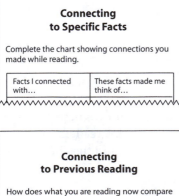

CONNECTING USING A WEB

Using a graphic organizer like a web or a mind map encourages students to explore a range of connections they may have to a text. Students may choose to include text-to-text, text-to-self, and text-to-world connections. They may form connections based on a wide range of experiences or prior knowledge. Using the graphic organizer allows students the opportunity to respond in a variety of ways (using pictures, words, sentences). Some students may choose to include evidence from the text in the form of examples, images, or quotes.

CONNECTING USING A VENN DIAGRAM FOR A VARIETY OF CONNECTIONS

This Venn diagram encourages students to form a number of connections to the text. They can identify similarities and differences to other texts, personal experiences, or knowledge they may have about the world. The graphic nature of the Venn diagram provides students with the opportunity to respond in a variety of ways. Graphic organizers can be as simple or as complex as the student chooses.

CONNECTING TO SPECIFIC TEXT

This task encourages students to identify elements in the text that sparked specific memories and various connections. Students record the specific event, fact, or feature of the text and describe the connections that they made from this. They may choose to include evidence from the text in the form of examples or quotes from the text.

CONNECTING USING A THREE-PART DIAGRAM

This three-part diagram provides areas for students to record text-to-text, text-to-self and text-to-world connections. Students may use the three-sided graphic organizer to record a variety of connections that they may make during reading. The open nature of this task provides students with a range of opportunities for responding. You will find that some students record numerous connections in each area of the diagram, whereas others choose to describe fewer connections in greater detail.

Connecting Task Descriptions: Non-Fiction

CONNECTING TO SPECIFIC FACTS

This task box invites students to record four facts they have read and to describe connections that they were able to form from them. They may think of a variety of connections based on their prior knowledge and personal experiences. Students may identify connections between their current reading and other books they have read, things they have seen on TV or online, or experiences that have contributed to their prior knowledge.

CONNECTING TO PREVIOUS READING

Forming text-to-text connections based on prior reading often helps to strengthen students' understanding of non-fiction material. When reflecting on what they have already read on a subject, students are usually able to form a deeper understanding of their text. Readers may find similarities between information on a subject, or even identify contradictions between texts. As students begin to evaluatively think about their reading, they are able to become much more critical readers. Critical readers are able to identify and analyze differences

Connecting to Personal Experiences

What does this story remind you of in your life?

_____
_____
_____
_____
_____
_____
_____
_____
_____

Connecting to Another Book

How is this book similar to another one that you have read?

_____
_____
_____
_____
_____
_____
_____
_____
_____
_____
_____

Connecting to a Specific Character

Choose one character in the book who is similar to you. Explain the similarities. (Remember to use examples from the text and your own life.)

_____
_____
_____
_____
_____
_____
_____
_____
_____

Connecting Using a Venn Diagram

Use a Venn diagram to compare this book to another one that you've read on a similar topic or by the same author.

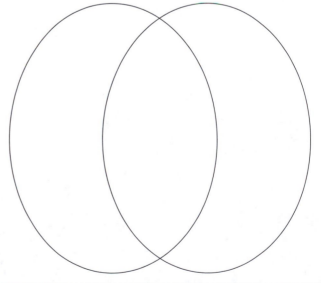

between texts and become more analytical about the information they encounter.

CONNECTING TO VALIDATE FACTS

Critically analyzing the facts presented in a text encourages students to think carefully about the information they are reading. Students describe ways in which they know the facts presented in the text are true. Through their personal connections or prior knowledge, students may be able to form some basis for validating the information in the text. Other readers may use non-fiction text features (e.g., illustrations, glossary) in order to support the facts presented in the text.

CONNECTING IDEAS WITHIN THE TEXT

Proficient readers are constantly searching for ways in which ideas connect together. In this task, students are invited to select two main ideas from the same text and discuss ways in which they are similar and different. An interesting point for discussion with a reader may be the student's perception as to why the author included the two ideas. What is the connection within the book between the two ideas?

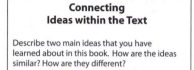

Connecting through Similar Experiences

Have you ever had an experience similar to one in the book? Describe what happened to you.

_____

_____

_____

_____

_____

_____

_____

Connecting to a Character through a Similar Experience

Does this text remind you of a problem that you had in your own life? How did you solve the problem?

_____

_____

_____

_____

Compare it to the problem in the story and how the characters solved their own problem.

_____

_____

_____

Connecting in a Variety of Ways

Describe ways in which you can personally connect to the book. You may think of similar characters, settings, or experiences.

_____

_____

_____

_____

_____

_____

_____

Connecting to Understand a Character's Actions

How does your experience of a similar situation help you to understand the character's actions?

_____

_____

_____

_____

_____

_____

_____

_____

Connecting
Using a Web

Create a web showing the connections you are able to make while reading. You may choose to put an important image, person, or event in the centre of the web.

Connecting
Using a Venn Diagram
for a Variety of Connections

Use the Venn diagram to make a text–text, text–self, or text–world connection. Record similarities and differences.

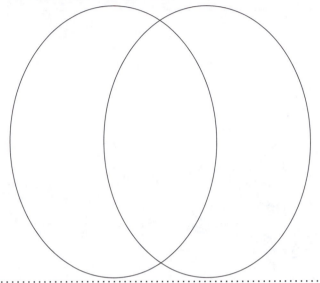

Connecting
to Specific Text

Did you form any special connections as you were reading? Describe a part of the book that reminded you of something else (another book, an interesting fact, or a personal connection; perhaps a person you know)

In the story:	Reminds me of:
_____	_____
_____	_____
_____	_____
_____	_____
_____	_____
_____	_____
_____	_____

Connecting
Using a Three-Part Diagram

Use the chart to record text–text, text–world, and text–self connections you made while reading.

Text–Text

Text–Self   Text–World

Connecting
to Specific Facts

Complete the chart showing connections you made while reading.

Facts I connected with…	These facts made me think of…

Connecting
to Previous Reading

How does what you are reading now compare to what you have already read on this topic?

_____

_____

_____

_____

_____

_____

_____

_____

_____

Connecting
to Validate Facts

Describe how you know that the facts in this book are true. Do you have any personal connections that support the ideas in the text? (Perhaps something else you've read, seen on TV, or personally experienced.)

_____

_____

_____

_____

_____

_____

_____

_____

Connecting
Ideas within the Text

Describe two main ideas that you have learned about in this book. How are the ideas similar? How are they different?

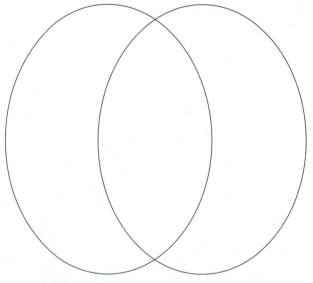

Rubric for Connecting

Skill	Level 1	Level 2	Level 3	Level 4
Record text-to-text, text-to-self and text-to-world connections	Few connections are recorded.	Some connections are recorded.	A variety of connections are recorded.	A variety of connections are recorded and clearly linked to passages from the text.
Use personal experiences to form connections to a text	Few personal experiences are described; connections to text may be unclear.	Personal experiences are described and somewhat connect to text.	Personal experiences are described and used as a basis for connections to the text.	Personal experiences are described, clearly connect to the text, and enhance student's understanding of the text.
Identify similarities and differences between texts and personal experiences	Few similarities and differences between text and personal experiences are described.	Some similarities and differences between text and personal experiences are described.	Many similarities and differences between text and personal experiences are described.	Many similarities and differences between text and personal experiences are clearly described; connections are made to key elements in the text.

Questioning

Proficient readers engage in an intricate dialogue with a text. Readers are not passive observers but active participants. Through asking questions and searching for answers in a text, students converse with the author. Each reader's questions are different, hence engagement with the text is a unique interaction for each reader. Two readers exposed to the same text may have completely different questions at any given point. Students may have questions about characters, the plot, an element in the book, or something that they found puzzling. At first, they may find it helpful to begin with a prompt such as "I wonder why…" or "I wonder how…" It is important to acknowledge a variety of question types, and try to refrain from answering the student's questions; rather, you should encourage students to search the text to find their own answers.

Initially it is difficult for students to ask questions of substance. In the context of school, children are accustomed to answering questions, not asking them. When students are first introduced to the challenge of expressing the questions they have while reading, they usually begin with simple concepts. Students require guidance to learn to ask deeper questions. Although students may initially ask questions with answers that seem obvious, with guidance they will gradually think of more complex and meaningful inquiries as they become competent at formulating questions.

As students become adept at formulating questions, they need to use the text to begin to answer them. If students keep a running record of their thoughts throughout the text, they discover how their thinking changes as they progress through the book.

The student samples shown on page 88 illustrate some of the different ways in which students can use questioning to strengthen their comprehension. In the first task, students are encouraged to keep a record of interesting questions that they would ask various characters; the sample here is on *Charlotte's Web* by E.B. White.

The other samples serve as a guide for students to organize their thinking when reading non-fiction texts. In the sample on *The Science of Plants* by Jonathan Bocknek, the student is given the opportunity to record things that he or she already knows (prior knowledge) and to formulate questions to address the things he or she still wishes to learn. The final sample can serve as a springboard for further inquiry, as students consider important questions that remain unanswered and think about a range of strategies and resources available to them to discover the answers; in this case, on the text *Helicopters* by Jeffrey Zuihlke.

Questioning Task Descriptions: Fiction

The following tasks provide a variety of opportunities for students to question their texts. Students may question the content of a text, use questioning to monitor their comprehension, and interact with the author through initiating a dialogue with the text. A number of opportunities are available for readers to respond in a variety of ways.

Generating questions helps students to fully engage in an intimate conversation with the author.

Younger students may need the support of a starting point or prompts in order to begin to formulate their questions. When we respond to their work, we are able to guide them into forming deeper and more meaningful questions.

The reproducible boxes on pages 91–94 can be copied and placed into Reading 8-Boxes for students' use.

Questioning

As you are reading, record questions that you would ask the various characters in the story.

Character	Question I would ask him/her
Fern	Why do you love the pig?
Charlotte	Why don't you go find the words?
Wilber	Where did you learn the tricks?
Animals	Do you want Wilber to stay?
Fern	Would you like to have kept Wilber?
Wilber	Who is your best freind?
Mr. Albern	Do you want to sell the pig for money?

Questioning Chart

As you read, add to the chart things you know and things you still want to learn.

Things I know	Things I still want to learn
-Plants can reproduce by seeds and pollenation.	-what is the most populated place of trees?
-Types (tumble weeds, sunflowers etc.	-How tall can trees grow up to?
-some plants a.k.a tropical plants can only be grown in tropical places! florida, california etc.	-Where is the tallest tree located?
-all plants have many cells, use sunlight to make food, and continue growing their entire life.	-What different colours can trees become?

Questioning

Write a new question that you have now that you would like to research further.

I wonder how come helicopters can lift very heavy loads and still be able to lift off the ground?

Explain how you would find the information to answer your question.

I will look on the Web! and then if I can't find the answer I will go to the library and get a book.

Questioning Using Prompts

As you are reading, record questions that you have.

I wonder ...

Questioning for Understanding

What were some of the questions you asked yourself while you were reading to make sure that you were understanding the book?

Questioning the Characters or Author

What are some questions you would like to ask the author or the characters in the book?

Questioning Using a Web

Create a web of questions you have while reading.

Questioning Using a Mind Map

Create a mind map of questions and answers you have while reading.

Answer:

Answer:

Question:

QUESTIONING USING PROMPTS

This task provides students with question prompts (*I wonder… What if…, Why did…*) to assist them in beginning to formulate questions. As young readers are starting to think about the text, they may form simple questions. The prompts are basic sentence starters that help students begin to express their questions about the text.

QUESTIONING FOR UNDERSTANDING

Students are encouraged to record questions that they used to monitor their understanding of the text. Some readers may record questions that directly connect to the content of the text, while others may think more about the mechanics of reading. Evaluating students' questions may provide insight into their thinking.

QUESTIONING THE CHARACTERS OR AUTHOR

Initiating a dialogue between the reader and the author is often accomplished when the reader is able to formulate questions about the text. In this task, students record questions that they may have for the characters or the author of the text. Some students may choose to later include the responses to the questions as they continue to read and learn more about the characters or text.

QUESTIONING USING A WEB

Using a web, students record a variety of questions they may have as they are reading. Some students may begin to form connections between questions and new ideas. A variety of responses are possible within the graphic nature of this task box, and students may include phrases, illustrations, or direct quotes from the text as they continue to think about the questions they have formulated.

QUESTIONING USING A MIND MAP

This task provides students with a framework for organizing their questions and answers. Using the graphic organizer, students record a variety of questions, and the answers as they become apparent. Some students may choose to include a variety of responses for their answers to their questions. They may include evidence from the text, diagrams, or descriptions of information from the text; or perhaps they are able to rely on their knowledge of the world in order to determine an appropriate response.

QUESTIONING AND LOOKING FOR ANSWERS

This task provides students with the opportunity to record questions they may have had and describe the ways they found the answers. It might not be possible for students to answer all of their questions, but they may be able to explain in greater detail how their question influenced their thinking about the text. Perhaps they have gained a greater insight into the text, or possibly their question has become the basis for a number of other questions that also remain unanswered. The goal is not to locate the answers to all questions, but for readers to begin to think deeply about the text in order to formulate complex questions that generate more thought about the text.

QUESTIONING VARIOUS CHARACTERS

Initiating a dialogue with the characters in a text enables readers to visualize them more effectively. Many fictional characters become very real in the reader's imaginations. With this task, readers formulate questions for different characters throughout the text. Some students may choose to ask many questions of a few characters, while other readers may have questions for many different characters. Readers may also have a variety of questions for the same character at different times throughout the text.

QUESTIONING: BEFORE, DURING, AND AFTER READING

This task allows students the opportunity to revisit their questions at various times through the text. Students record their questions before, during, and after reading. When reading a shorter text, students may use the book in its entirety; however, as is often the case with proficient readers, they may be engaged in a much longer text. In this case, students may choose to record their questioning of certain section of the text (perhaps one chapter). Some questions may remain unanswered; however, students are encouraged to deepen their thinking about the text, and to describe new questions that are the result of thinking about their initial question.

QUESTIONING: RECORDING AND REFLECTING ON QUESTIONS

The open-ended nature of this task allows for students to formulate a range of questions as they are reading. Students are encouraged to remain cognizant of their questions and they may record the answers they might later discover to their questions. Some questions may remain unanswered, some answers may be easily apparent, some questions will serve only to generate further questions, and others may be answered much later in the text. All questions are valid, as they succeed in achieving the goal of initiating a dialogue between the reader and the text.

QUESTIONING: RAVIN' REPORTER

In this task, students are invited to think in role as a reporter. If they were given the opportunity to interview one of the main characters in the book, what questions would they ask? Students are also asked to consider the ways in which the character might respond to these questions.

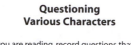

Questioning and Looking for Answers

What questions did you ask yourself while reading that helped you to understand the book better? How did you find the answers?

Questions I had	How I found the answers

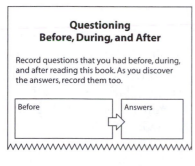

Questioning Various Characters

As you are reading, record questions that you would ask the various characters in the story.

Characters	Questions I would ask him/her

Questioning Before, During, and After

Record questions that you had before, during, and after reading this book. As you discover the answers, record them too.

Before	Answers

Questioning Recording and Reflecting on Questions

As you are reading, record questions that you have. Later, if you discover the answers, record them too.

Questioning Ravin' Reporter

Pretend that you are a reporter interviewing one of the characters in the book. What questions would you ask? How do you think the character might respond?

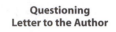

Questioning
Just One Question

If you could ask the author or characters just one question about this book, what would be the most important thing you'd want to know?

Questioning
Letter to the Author

Write a brief letter to the author asking him/her to answer some questions that you have about the book. For example, you may be wondering why he/she chose a certain

Questioning
for Further Inquiry

Write a new question that you have now that you would like to research further.

Questioning Chart

As you read, add to the chart things you know and things you still want to learn.

Things I know	Things I still want to learn

Questioning (FQR)

Complete the FQR chart below. Select three important facts from the text. For each fact, record a question you have about it and your response to either the fact or your question.

Questioning
Research Report

If you were using this book to start a research report, what are three questions that you could use to find out more about this subject? Record some of the things you have already learned by reading this book.

QUESTIONING: JUST ONE QUESTION

In this task, students are asked to think of one question that they would like to ask the author or one of the characters. They are then required to justify their thinking by explaining why they think this is the most important thing that they would like revealed to them. The narrow focus of this task requires that students be quite precise in their thinking.

QUESTIONING: LETTER TO THE AUTHOR

In this task, students write a letter to the author in order to express their questions about the text. Students may have questions about the setting of the text, or the actions or nature of a specific character, or a specific event that remains unresolved or seems confusing. Sophisticated readers might begin to question the underlying themes or bigger ideas (such as fairness, discrimination, disloyalty, etc.) in the book.

Questioning Task Descriptions: Non-Fiction

QUESTIONING FOR FURTHER INQUIRY

When reading non-fiction, students often generate questions that may lead to further research. In this task, students consider what information they would still be interested in finding out, as well as explaining strategies that may aid in locating it. This task can serve as a springboard for questions (*What you want to know? How you will find out?*) that introduce students to research skills.

QUESTIONING CHART

Activating prior knowledge before reading may be the source for generating questions for further inquiry. In this task, students record things that they know about the topic of their text, and record things that they still wish to learn. If students continue to add to this list throughout their reading, their knowledge will expand, and their questions may change or get answered.

QUESTIONING: FQR

Using the chart, students record three interesting facts from the text. For each fact they generate a question. Finally, students consider their response to their question. For example, a student may record the fact that polar bears are white; a question about this fact may be "Why are they white?"; finally, the response may be that polar bears need to be able to camouflage in their habitat.

QUESTIONING: RESEARCH REPORT

In this task, students are asked to formulate three questions for further inquiry. After recording their questions, students record things that they have already learned from the book in response to these questions. Students may use point-form notes and record as many ideas as possible for each question. As a possible extension, the student's notes from this task would easily form the basis of a short writing assignment; e.g., a three-paragraph report, summary, or reflection on the text.

Questioning
Using Prompts

As you are reading, record questions that you have.

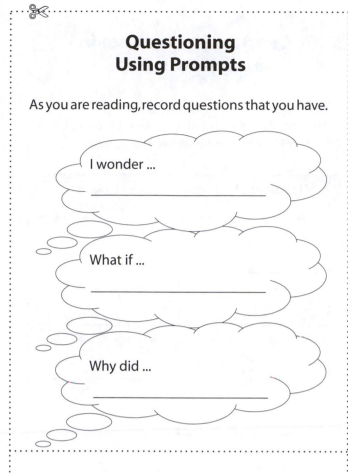

I wonder …

What if …

Why did …

Questioning
for Understanding

What were some of the questions you asked yourself while you were reading to make sure that you were understanding the book?

1. _____

_____

_____

2. _____

_____

_____

3. _____

_____

_____

Questioning the Characters
or Author

What are some questions you would like to ask the author or the characters in the book?

_____

_____

_____

_____

_____

_____

_____

_____

Questioning Using a Web

Create a web of questions you have while reading.

I wonder …

Questioning Using a Mind Map

Create a mind map of questions and answers you have while reading.

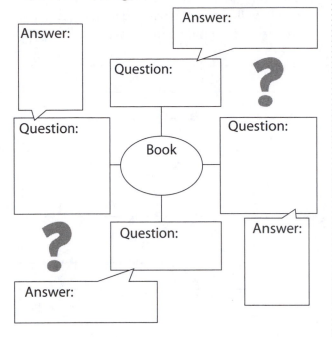

Questioning and Looking for Answers

What questions did you ask yourself while reading that helped you to understand the book better? How did you find the answers?

Questions I had	How I found the answers

Questioning Various Characters

As you are reading, record questions that you would ask the various characters in the story.

Characters	Questions I would ask him/her

Questioning Before, During, and After

Record questions that you had before, during, and after reading this book. As you discover the answers, record them too.

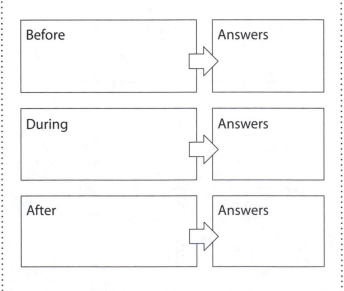

Questioning
Recording and Reflecting on Questions

As you are reading, record questions that you have. Later, if you discover the answers, record them too.

_____

_____

_____

_____

_____

_____

_____

_____

Questioning
Ravin' Reporter

Pretend that you are a reporter interviewing one of the characters in the book. What questions would you ask? How do you think the character might respond?

_____

_____

_____

_____

_____

_____

_____

_____

_____

Questioning
Just One Question

If you could ask the author or characters just one question about this book, what would be the most important thing you'd want to know?

_____

_____

_____

_____

Why would you want to know this?

_____

_____

_____

Questioning
Letter to the Author

Write a brief letter to the author asking him/her to answer some questions that you have about the book. For example, you may be wondering why he/she chose a certain setting, or why a character behaves in a specific way, or about an issue that remains unresolved and seems confusing.

_____ ,

_____

_____

_____

_____

_____

_____

_____

Questioning
for Further Inquiry

Write a new question that you have now that you would like to research further.

_____

_____

_____

_____

Explain how you would find the information to answer your question.

_____

_____

_____

_____

Questioning Chart

As you read, add to the chart things you know and things you still want to learn.

Things I know	Things I still want to learn

Questioning
FQR

Complete the FQR chart below. Select three important facts from the text. For each fact, record a question you have about it and your response to either the fact or your question.

Fact	**Q**uestion	**R**esponse

Questioning
Research Report

If you were using this book to start a research report, what are three questions that you could use to find out more about this subject? Record some of the things you have already learned by reading this book.

Question for Inquiry	Things I learned from this book

Rubric for Questioning

Skill	Level 1	Level 2	Level 3	Level 4
Record areas of curiosity or confusion while reading	Student rarely reflects on his/her own understanding of texts and rarely records areas of confusion or curiosity.	Student sometimes reflects on his/her own understanding of texts and records areas of confusion or curiosity.	Student effectively reflects on his/her own understanding of texts and records areas of confusion or curiosity.	Student consistently reflects on his/her own understanding of texts and records areas of confusion or curiosity.
Formulate questions to initiate dialogue with text	Few questions are recorded while reading text.	Some questions are recorded while reading text.	Many questions are recorded while reading text.	Many thoughtful questions are recorded while reading text.
Ask questions before, during, and after reading a variety of texts.	Few questions are recorded at different stages of reading.	Some questions are recorded at various stages of reading.	Many questions are recorded at various stages of reading.	Many creative questions are recorded at various stages of reading.
Ask questions and formulate answers using information from the text	Student is beginning to reflect on questions recorded while reading, and to consider answers to these questions using information from the text and his/her own ideas.	Student occasionally reflects on questions recorded while reading, and considers answers to these questions using information from the text and his/her own ideas.	Student reflects on questions recorded while reading, and considers answers to these questions using information from the text and his/her own ideas.	Student independently reflects on questions recorded while reading, and considers answers to these questions using information from the text and his/her own ideas.

Visualizing

When we speak to students of visualizing, we often tell them to create pictures in their mind or to imagine the story like a movie. Although it is important for students to fully utilize their sense of vision, their other senses are just as crucial. Visualizing with all their senses increases students' understanding of the text. Imagining the tone of a character's voice, the smell of dirty gym socks, or the feeling of a cold damp sweat or the hair on the back of your neck tingling are all visualizations that help readers gain deeper insight into a text.

Adrienne Gear (2006) considers visualizing the "sister to imagination," the critical difference being the source for the images. Gear states that when we are imagining, the images created come from within; whereas, when visualizing, the source for the images is the text. The ability to visualize is also strongly connected with one's prior knowledge and experiences. It becomes important for students to have a good understanding of key ideas in order to effectively formulate images in their mind. Students who have never previously encountered certain things will have greater difficulty visualizing them. When introducing and practicing visualizing, it is important to choose books with things that students are familiar with. It is also effective to draw students' attention to descriptive language that helps to create mental images.

The task boxes that reinforce visualizing are probably the ones that are most enjoyed by the students. They thoroughly enjoy sharing their visualizations with others and are usually eager to complete these tasks in great detail. As our students use their mind's eye to imagine the intricate details of different texts, it is important that we encourage them to use more than one of their senses. Although visualization typically refers to things that we can see, we need to remind our students to actively use all of their senses to become fully engaged with the text.

In the first sample on page 97, the student is given the opportunity to illustrate and describe a favorite character; in this case, Franklin from *Franklin Plays Hockey* by Brian Lasenby. Although this is a simple task, it is very versatile, as the expectations of the task could become progressively more demanding with older readers. Perhaps more proficient readers could include direct evidence from the text in the form of a quote to support their illustration.

In the second task box, students consider many different dimensions of one main idea in a text. The student has chosen a descriptive passage from *Charlotte's Web* by E.B. White and considers its sensory impact: What does it look like? Sound like? Feel like? Encouraging students to use their imagination in partnership with the text will help them to develop stronger mental images.

Finally, this sample on the text *Bugs of Ontario* by John Acorn and Ian Sheldon shows how students can create a detailed diagram to explain a main idea from a non-fiction text. They should include as much information as possible in the form of labels, captions, a title, and a detailed illustration.

Visualizing Task Descriptions: Fiction

The following tasks are designed to provide students with a variety of opportunities to visualize text while reading. Due to the graphic nature of this skill, students are encouraged to respond in many creative ways, including using pictures, diagrams, and descriptive words or phrases.

Drawing students' attention to particularly descriptive phrases or words will aid their ability to visualize new ideas.

Visualizing tasks are provided for both fiction and non-fiction texts in order to effectively target the range of concepts in each genre.

The reproducible boxes on pages 99–101 can be copied and placed into Reading 8-Boxes for students' use.

Visualizing

Draw a picture of your favourite character in the story. Write words to describe them.

HE IS FAST AND HE LIKES to PLAY HOCKEY

Visualizing

Choose a particularly descriptive passage of the book. Record things that you were able to visualize as you were reading. Use as many of your senses as possible.

See / Hear / Smell / Taste / Feel

10. Visualizing
Creating a Diagram

Create a diagram to explain something from the text. Use labels to explain your thinking.

A Yellow Jacket

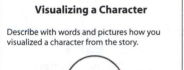

Visualizing a Character

Describe with words and pictures how you visualized a character from the story.

Visualizing a Favorite Character

Draw a picture of your favorite character in the story. Write words to describe that character.

Visualizing with Sight and Sound

What are some things that you can see or hear in your mind as you are reading the book?

Visualizing with Sight, Sound, and Smell

What are some things you could see, hear, or smell while reading?

Visualizing Using all Five Senses

Choose a particularly descriptive passage of the book. Record things that you were able to visualize as you were reading. Use as many of your senses as possible.

VISUALIZING A CHARACTER

Young readers are often able to visualize characters from their stories. In this task, they draw and label a picture of one of the characters. Some students may include words and phrases around the character to support their illustration. Readers may include information that describes the character's physical appearance and their personality.

VISUALIZING A FAVORITE CHARACTER

In this task, students choose their favorite character to represent visually. They may also include written information to describe this character. Stronger readers may include evidence from the text to support their thinking, in the form of an example or direct quote from the text.

VISUALIZING WITH SIGHT AND SOUND

Students use the graphic organizer to provide examples of how they visualized portions of the text using their senses of sight and sound. They may describe the appearance of a specific stetting, character, or event in the text. Creative readers may find interesting ways of responding to this task. Some students may include images, words, phrases, quotes, or other ways of conveying their thinking about the text.

VISUALIZING WITH SIGHT, SOUND, AND SMELL

This task is an extension of the previous task. In this task, students use the graphic organizer to record things that they could virtually see, hear, and smell while reading.

VISUALIZING WITH ALL FIVE SENSES

Students choose a particularly descriptive passage from the text and record things they were able to visualize using all of their senses while reading. They may need to envision themselves in the role of one of the characters in order to fully apply all five senses.

**Visualizing
Create a Magazine Advertisement**

Create a magazine advertisement to promote the book. Remember to include the title, the author, an illustration, and an interesting caption about the book.

**Visualizing
Celebrity Characters**

If you were in charge of turning the book into a movie, which celebrities would play the different characters? Describe why you think each celebrity is the best match for the character.

Visualizing a Specific Event

Use the space below to draw an image that you visualized while reading. Include evidence from the text that supports your picture.

**Visualizing
Creating a Diagram**

Create a diagram to explain something from the text. Use labels to explain your thinking.

**Visualizing
Looks Like, Sounds Like, Feels Like**

Choose an important idea from the text and describe it with pictures and words. What does it *look like*, *sound like*, and *feel like*?

VISUALIZING: CREATE A MAGAZINE ADVERTISEMENT

Students consider an alternative form of media to promote their book. They combine their knowledge of a non-fiction book with the graphic nature of a familiar and popular text form to create a magazine advertisement. In order to complete this task, students are asked to consider their text from a different perspective—it is not only a book to be read, but a product to be sold. By creating a magazine advertisement, students are required to consider the audience the book is suited for, a graphic representation of the book, and a phrase intended to capture the reader's attention.

VISUALIZING: CELEBRITY CHARACTERS

Many students naturally form connections between books and movies. In this task, students consider which celebrities would fit the roles of the characters in the book. They think about the best match for the character and to justify their choice. Some students may choose to find pictures of their favorite celebrity in magazines or on the Internet to complete their task box.

VISUALIZING A SPECIFIC EVENT

Some portions of texts are more vividly described than others, and leave readers with a clear mental image of the event. This task encourages students to select a particularly descriptive passage and illustrate the image that was generated in their mind. Readers can provide support for their illustration in the form of words, phrases, or direct quotes from the text.

Visualizing Task Descriptions: Non-Fiction

VISUALIZING: CREATING A DIAGRAM

Students create a diagram to represent a concept they have read about. They may include labels to explain their thinking. Some students may choose to apply their reading to an image that they have encountered in the text, while others may be able to create an original representation of the facts in the book.

VISUALIZING: LOOKS LIKE, SOUNDS LIKE, FEELS LIKE

Students select one main idea from the text and use their senses to describe what it may look like, sound like, or feel like. Students may record their thinking with pictures, words, phrases, sentences, or quotes from the text. Creative readers may find a variety of ways to respond to this task.

Visualizing a Character

Describe with words and pictures how you visualized a character from the story.

Visualizing a Favorite Character

Draw a picture of your favorite character in the story. Write words to describe that character.

Visualizing with Sight and Sound

What are some things that you can see or hear in your mind as you are reading the book?

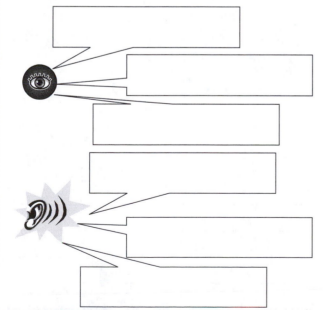

Visualizing with Sight, Sound, and Smell

What are some things you could see, hear, or smell while reading?

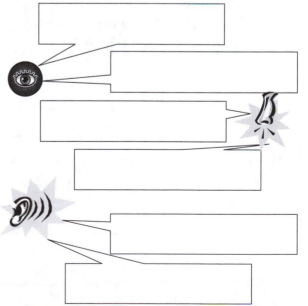

Visualizing
Using all Five Senses

Choose a particularly descriptive passage of the book. Record things that you were able to visualize as you were reading. Use as many of your senses as possible.

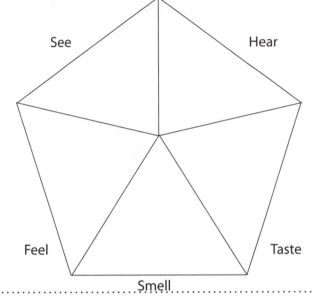

Visualizing
Create a Magazine Advertisement

Create a magazine advertisement to promote the book. Remember to include the title, the author, an illustration, and an interesting caption about the book.

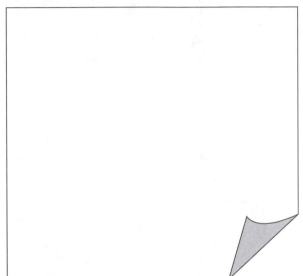

Visualizing
Celebrity Characters

If you were in charge of turning the book into a movie, which celebrities would play the different characters? Describe why you think each celebrity is the best match for the character.

Now Starring ...

Visualizing a Specific Event

Use the space below to draw an image that you visualized while reading. Include evidence from the text that supports your picture.

Visualizing
Creating a Diagram

Create a diagram to explain something from the
text. Use labels to explain your thinking.

Visualizing
Looks Like, Sounds Like, Feels Like

Choose an important idea from the text and
describe it with pictures and words. What does it
look like, *sound like*, and *feel like*?

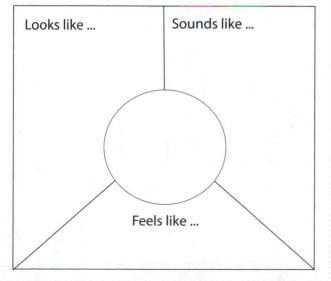

Rubric for Visualizing

Skill	Level 1	Level 2	Level 3	Level 4
Use writing to describe mental images	Writing is vague and does not clearly describe mental images constructed while reading.	Writing somewhat describes mental images constructed while reading.	Writing effectively describes mental images constructed while reading.	Writing vividly describes mental images constructed while reading.
Use imagery from the text to create visual images (illustrations)	Few images from the text are clearly represented with illustrations and ideas.	Illustrations and ideas somewhat represent images conveyed in the text.	Illustrations and ideas clearly represent images conveyed in the text.	Illustrations and ideas clearly represent images conveyed in the text; some evidence may be included to support the student's thinking.
Identify sensory words and images while reading	Few sensory words and images are included	Some sensory words and images are included.	Sensory words, phrases, and images are included.	Many sensory words, phrases, and images are included.
Provide evidence from the text to support images	Little or vague evidence from the text is provided to support illustration.	Some evidence from the text is provided to support illustration	Appropriate evidence from the text is provided to support illustration.	Student provides more than one relevant piece of evidence to support illustration.

Inferring

Inferring is the ability to recognize the theme or moral of a story, identify the feelings of characters, and generally "read between the lines." Readers detect the subtleties and nuances provided by the author that lead them to think in a certain way.

Authors provide many opportunities for readers to read between the lines. This is a very challenging task for younger readers, as they are such literal thinkers. Young children struggle with inferential and figurative language, and may be confused when encountering these types of phrases in their reading.

Inferring is often used when identifying the theme of the story. If students learn to read critically for the theme, moral, or lesson in a story, they become more able to filter through erroneous information and break the story in to its most rudimentary elements. Students can learn to identify the lesson or unifying theme in the text by trying to summarize the most important ideas in the story in one sentence or even one word. The more exposure students gain to a variety of genres of books the larger repertoire of knowledge they will have to draw on in order to find the underlying themes.

As readers, we tend to connect with characters through our own experiences or emotions. Sophisticated readers are able to easily draw conclusions about how characters feel based on cues from the author. Younger readers require more guidance in this area. If the author does not say that someone is sad, for example, students may not realize that this is so. Have you ever completed reading aloud a moving picture book and cleared the lump in your throat, only to glance around the room and find your students staring in wonder at your emotional reaction to the text? Perhaps the youngsters had failed to find the author's purpose, failed to identify the mood, or failed to feel empathy for a character. We feel empathy for others because we can identify feelings, and our emotions may be reactions to the inferences we make as we read. Directing students' attention to such cues as body language, tone of voice, or actions may help them to make these inferences with greater ease.

Finally, be patient when teaching students to make inferences. There will always be the few who will still feel that they "just don't get it." Inferences are personal interpretations of a text; not all readers will make the same inferences, and some students won't get it until the author "hits them over the head with

Inferring is particularly challenging for English Language Learners and some students with learning disabilities, as they face the double difficulty of understanding each word in addition to trying to determine a seemingly obscure meaning.

The Character's Actions sample is on *Goldilocks and the Three Bears,* retold by Jan Brett; the sample on the right is on *Rover Saves Christmas* by Roddy Doyle.

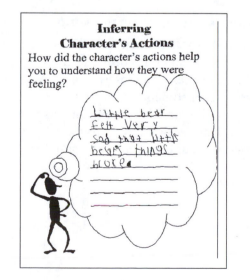

Inferring
Character's Actions

How did the character's actions help you to understand how they were feeling?

Little bear felt very sad that little bear's things broke

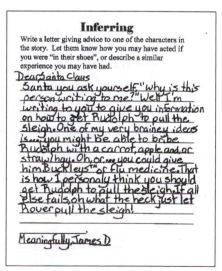

Inferring

Write a letter giving advice to one of the characters in the story. Let them know how you may have acted if you were "in their shoes", or describe a similar experience you may have had.

Dear Santa Claus
Santa you ask yourself "why is this person writing to me?" Well I'm writing to you to give you information on how to get Rudolph to pull the sleigh. One of my very brainey ideas is you might be able to bribe Rudolph with a carrot, apple and or straw/hay. Oh, or... you could give him Buckleys™ or flu medicine. That is how I personaly think you should get Rudolph to pull the sleigh. If all else fails, oh what the heck just let Rover pull the sleigh!

Meaningfully, James D

it"—and that's okay. We all develop our internal conversations with text at different rates, and some readers will find making inferences more challenging than others.

The tasks intended to help students strengthen their understanding of inferring start with concrete concepts and lead into more abstract thinking. For example, the first sample on page 103 asks students to examine how the character's actions helped the reader to understand their feelings. Many students are able to understand the subtleties of body language when interacting with their peers and adults. They are often able to determine how someone is feeling based on the way they are acting. It is a bit of a challenge for students to transfer this understanding to texts. By beginning with simple texts and simpler prompts, students will begin to discover the importance of being able to judge character's feelings from their actions. Younger students may find concrete examples of how characters' actions convey their feelings (he laughed… so he was happy; or he pouted… so he was sad). Encouraging students to form these initial connections between actions and emotions will strengthen their ability to make inferences.

The second sample invites students to provide advice to the characters in the story describing a similar experience that they may have had. By asking students to describe the ways they may have acted if faced with a similar situation, they are envisioning themselves in the role of a character.

Inferring Task Descriptions

Inferential tasks ask readers to think beyond the literal content of the text and form conclusions and opinions. Determining character's emotions or motivation, identifying underlying themes or lessons, and placing the reader's self in another's shoes are all based on the reader's ability to make inferences.

Inferring often calls upon readers to think of the text as a whole. They need to move away from individual incidents and actions, and consider the overall lessons or morals that are implied in the text. They need to search for underlying themes throughout the text and then provide evidence to support their thinking. This level of inferring is quite complex.

The reproducible boxes on pages 106–107 can be copied and placed into Reading 8-Boxes for students' use.

Inferring a Character's Feelings

How do you think the main character feels at the end of the story? What are some clues that made you think this?

Inferring from a Character's Actions

How did the character's actions help you to understand how he or she was feeling?

INFERRING A CHARACTER'S FEELINGS

Readers consider the ways in which a character may feel at the end of the story. They should think about a variety of clues that may lead them to their conclusion. Readers may provide evidence that refers to a character's actions, words, or other clues that may indicate their feelings.

INFERRING FROM A CHARACTER'S ACTIONS

In this task, students analyze ways in which a character's actions enabled the reader to understand his or her feelings. Students may draw on a range of personal experiences when interpreting the actions of characters. It is sometimes challenging for students to understand when a character may seem conflicted by having mixed emotions. Strong readers may be able to think about a character in a multi-dimensional way, recognizing that it is possible for one person to experience a number of emotions simultaneously.

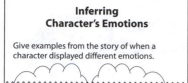

**Inferring
Character's Emotions**

Give examples from the story of when a character displayed different emotions.

**Inferring
Letter in Role**

Pretend you are one of the characters. Write a letter to someone describing what has happened so far, how you are feeling, and what you think might happen next.

**Inferring a Character's
Thoughts**

Are there times when you can determine what characters are thinking from their words and actions? Describe one of these times. Provide evidence from the text to support your answer.

**Inferring
In a Character's Shoes**

If you were the main character, how would you feel and what would you do?

**Inferring
Offering Advice**

Write a letter giving advice to a character. You can suggest actions the character might take, or reveal some important information.

**Inferring
Lessons Learned**

What lessons can you learn from the story? How does the author teach you these lessons without stating them directly?

INFERRING: CHARACTER'S EMOTIONS

Readers provide three examples of a character displaying different emotions. Considering the changes a character undergoes throughout a story enables readers to have a stronger sense of the character's development. This graphic organizer allows students the opportunity to respond in a variety of creative ways. Some students may choose to respond with words, pictures, or examples. They may provide evidence from the text, or even use thought/speech bubbles to clarify the character's thought in an illustration.

INFERRING: LETTER IN ROLE

This task allows students to think and write in role as one of the characters in the story. Readers write a letter to someone describing what has happened so far, how they are feeling, and what they think might happen next. Students may choose to write their letter to another of the book's characters, forming meaningful connections between the two.

INFERRING A CHARACTER'S THOUGHTS

Often we are able to understand the social nuances that lead us to conclusions about the thoughts and feelings of others. We interpret another's body language, tone of voice, and facial expression. As readers, we also become savvy at identifying and interpreting subtleties throughout the text to infer a character's thoughts, emotions, and motivations. In this task, readers describe times they used the character's words and actions to better understand a character's thoughts. Evidence may be presented in the form of an example from the story or even a direct quote from the text.

INFERRING: IN A CHARACTER'S SHOES

In this task, readers consider the actions of the character by placing themselves in his or her shoes. Students are asked how they would feel and act if they were the main character. It would be best if students consider a critical turning point or climactic moment in the plot at which to "switch places" with the character. The wealth of prior knowledge and experiences that a reader brings to a text greatly influences their thoughts.

INFERRING: OFFERING ADVICE

Everyone loves to give their "two cents' worth." No matter what the situation, we all seem to be ready with some unsolicited advice. In this task, readers provide one of the characters with some advice. They write a letter to one of the characters, letting them know how they may have acted or describing a similar event. Often readers feel aptly equipped to face the dilemmas faced by the characters and are eager to share their thoughts and opinions. It becomes interesting for readers to continue reading to see if their advice may have aided the characters.

INFERRING: LESSONS LEARNED

In this task, students look at the story in its entirety and identify an important lesson that they learned from the text. They are also asked to describe the ways in which the author conveyed these lessons without stating them directly. For example, students may form connections between ideas at the beginning and end of the book, examine the ways in which characters evolve and develop throughout the text, or consider the resolution of a conflict.

Inferring a Character's Feelings

How do you think the main character feels at the end of the story? What are some clues that made you think this?

_____

_____

_____

_____

_____

_____

_____

_____

_____

Inferring from a Character's Actions

How did the character's actions help you to understand how he or she was feeling?

Inferring Character's Emotions

Give examples from the story of when a character displayed different emotions.

Inferring Letter in Role

Pretend you are one of the characters. Write a letter to someone describing what has happened so far, how you are feeling, and what you think might happen next.

_____ ,

_____

_____

_____

_____

_____

_____

_____

Inferring a Character's Thoughts

Are there times when you can determine what characters are thinking from their words and actions? Describe one of these times. Provide evidence from the text to support your answer.

_____

_____

_____

_____

_____

_____

_____

Inferring In a Character's Shoes

If you were the main character, how would you feel and what would you do?

_____

_____

_____

_____

_____

_____

_____

_____

Inferring Offering Advice

Write a letter giving advice to a character. You can suggest actions the character might take, or reveal some important information.

_____

_____

_____

_____

_____

_____

_____

_____

Inferring Lessons Learned

What lessons can you learn from the story? How does the author teach you these lessons without stating them directly?

_____

_____

_____

_____

_____

_____

_____

_____

Rubric for Inferring

Skill	Level 1	Level 2	Level 3	Level 4
Identify theme or main idea of text	Theme is not clearly stated or is not supported by the main ideas of the text.	Theme is somewhat stated and is partially supported by the main ideas of the text.	Theme is stated and is supported with some evidence from the text.	Theme is clearly identified and thoroughly supported with evidence from the text.
Use evidence from the text to infer feelings/emotions of characters	Main characters' feelings are not identified; little or no evidence from the text is provided.	Main characters' feelings are somewhat described using stated and implied evidence from the text.	Main characters' feelings are described using stated and implied evidence from the text.	Main characters' feelings are clearly described using stated and implied evidence from the text.
Identify the point of view presented in texts and suggest possible alternative perspectives	Point of view and alternative perspectives are unclear.	Point of view is discussed and alternative perspectives considered.	Point of view is thoughtfully discussed and alternative perspectives considered.	Point of view is thoughtfully discussed and alternative perspectives considered based on evidence from the text.
Describe lessons learned from the story and justify thinking with evidence from the text	Student finds it challenging to identify important lessons; there is little evidence from the text to support his/her thinking.	Lessons are stated and somewhat supported with evidence from the text.	Important lessons are clearly stated and supported with evidence from the text.	Important lessons are clearly stated and supported with a number of examples and evidence form the text.

Predicting

Predicting is closely linked to inferring. A prediction is a guess based on existing knowledge of the text. Readers make predictions using their prior knowledge, their understanding of the world, and their previous experiences with similar texts. As readers, we turn pages with excitement, gasp with satisfaction, and sigh with dismay as we discover whether our predictions were correct or not. Engagement in reading is high when we are actively participating in the plot and eagerly thinking about what will happen next. When we make predictions, we are continuing our dialogue with the text. We are formulating our own ideas and comparing them to those of the author. Every reader, regardless of age, loves the satisfaction that comes with the final revelation that they had accurately predicted.

While reading a series of mystery books with some students, we engaged in a rather heated discussion on how to narrow the list of suspects in order to formulate predictions. Using all of the author's clues, directions, and perceived misdirections, students were eager to determine whether they had correctly guessed the outcome of the book. Students looked for similarities between books of the same genre or by the same author, drawing on a wide range of prior knowledge and personal experiences. As they continued to read to the exciting climax of the story, the room was filled with loud *ah-ha*s, "Oh my gosh!" "I knew it!" "I told you so!" and "No way… I never saw that coming… I have to read this part again." The readers were completely immersed in the book, excited about the conclusion.

Predicting task boxes allow readers to record their predictions, both at particular points in the text (such as the climax of the story) and through their reading. They are invited to use a range of evidence upon which to base their predictions. When students keep a running record of their predictions, they can return to them later and determine whether they were correct or not. Some students enjoy reflecting on predictions that they made earlier and revising them once they have learned more from the text.

It is important for students to realize that a *right* prediction is not synonymous with a *right* answer. As long as predictions are based on information from the text, any and all predictions are valid—even the ones that initially may seem a little obscure.

The Predicting at the Climax task is on the text *Storm is Coming* by Heather Tekavec; the chart tracks a reader's predictions of *Measle and the Wrathmonk* by Ian Ogilvy.

Nicole 11

1. Predicting at the Climax

Choose an exciting part of the story and predict what you think will happen next.

I think there is a thunder storm that will continue going on in the book and one of the cows did not make it into the farm because in the pictures I see a thunder storm and when I looked on the back of the book I saw on the back of the book a cow walking to the farm.

Predicting

Use the chart below to track your predictions. Record predictions that you make as you are reading, and later check whether you were correct or not.

Prediction	Correct
I think the "thing" in the rafters is a cross between a bat and a rat.	no it is only a bat
I think the "thing" in the rafter is going to raid the mini town.	yes Measle almost died
I predict that when Measle finds out what the "thing" in the rafters is he'll faint.	no he screamed
I think if they drink the water in the fountain it will make them feel better.	no the water was fake
I think that they will slide down the table leg and venture into unknown land.	no they would die
I predict that at the end of the book they will defeat Basil.	yes the house collapsed

Predicting Task Descriptions

The reproducible boxes on page 111 can be copied and placed into Reading 8-Boxes for students' use.

Predicting at the Climax

Choose an exciting part of the story and predict what you think will happen next.

_____

_____

**Predicting
Using Early Clues**

Look carefully at the title and the beginning of the story. What do you think the story will be about? Explain your predictions with ideas from your past reading and your own

---

**Predicting
Monitoring Predictions**

Record your predictions as you are reading. Indicate whether your prediction was correct.

I predict ...	I was correct	I was not

Predicting Using Evidence

Record predictions that you make as you are reading. Beside each, include the evidence from the book that led you to your prediction. You may include a quote from the book (and page number), or describe a particular event.

These task boxes allow students opportunities to form predictions, and revisit and evaluate their predictions later in the text. Some tasks require that students provide evidence from the text in order to support their predictions.

PREDICTING AT THE CLIMAX

Readers are invited to choose an exciting part of the story and make a prediction about what they think might happen next. Young readers may need help with identifying an appropriate point at which to stop and record their prediction. Some students relish the opportunity to later return to their prediction and identify whether they had predicted accurately. During conferences, ask students to reflect on their predictions and identify the clues in the text that led them to make those particular predictions.

PREDICTING USING EARLY CLUES

Through an examination of the text elements (the title and the beginning of the book), students make early predictions about the text. They can record what they think the story will be about and justify their thinking using their prior knowledge and past experiences. This task introduces students to the importance of using the clues in the book as a basis for forming predictions. A prediction is not a "stab in the dark," but rather an educated guess based on evidence in the text.

PREDICTING: MONITORING PREDICTIONS

During this task students record their predictions, and later refer to them to determine if they were correct. It is helpful for students to complete this task over a longer period of time, as they will have a greater opportunity to discover if they were successful with their predictions. Some students enjoy the opportunity to revisit earlier predictions and revise them as they discover more information in the text.

PREDICTING USING EVIDENCE

Readers are required to provide evidence to support their thinking. This task asks students to record their predictions and justify their thinking with evidence from the text. Some students may choose to provide evidence in the form of an example from the story, or they may provide a direct quote to support their prediction.

Predicting at the Climax

Choose an exciting part of the story and predict what you think will happen next.

_____

_____

_____

_____

_____

_____

_____

_____

_____

_____

Predicting Using Early Clues

Look carefully at the title and the beginning of the story. What do you think the story will be about? Explain your predictions with ideas from your past reading and your own experiences.

_____

_____

_____

_____

_____

_____

_____

_____

Predicting
Monitoring Predictions

Record your predictions as you are reading. Indicate whether your prediction was correct.

I predict ...	I was correct	I was not correct

Predicting Using Evidence

Record predictions that you make as you are reading. Beside each, include the evidence from the book that led you to your prediction. You may include a quote from the book (and page number), or describe a particular event.

Prediction	Evidence from the Book

Rubric for Predicting

Skill	Level 1	Level 2	Level 3	Level 4
Make reasonable predictions based on evidence presented in the text	Predictions are unclear or not supported by the text.	Predictions are somewhat based on the text.	Predictions are reasonable and based on the text.	Predictions are creative, well-developed, and supported by the text.
Reassess predictions as new information is read	Predictions are not revised or reassessed as new information is read.	Predictions are partially revised as new information is read.	Predictions are logically assessed and revised accordingly.	Predictions are logically assessed as new information is thoughtfully considered.
Provide evidence from the text to support predictions	Little or no evidence is given to support predictions.	Predictions are somewhat supported by evidence from the text.	Predictions are supported by evidence from the text.	Predictions are clearly supported by evidence from the text.

We need to help students see the big picture and determine the most important ideas.

Determining Importance

When students determine the importance of a text, they are able to identify and sequence the main ideas. They are able to find the "big picture" rather than focus on the obscure details.

When our five-year-old son returned from watching a movie, I asked the obvious first question: "What was it about?" He launched into a very descriptive monologue about the funniest parts, and paused only to illustrate these through dramatic movement. He laughed, acted, rolled on the floor, and shared random bits of information from the movie. He used phrases like "you know what else happened…" and "it was so funny when…" His answer to my question lasted a complete ten minutes, and after his response, I still had little idea about the basic plot of the movie. I did however, recognize that there were many portions that he found hilarious, as he could not describe them to me without bursting into fits of laughter. He was so distracted by the various scenes of the movie that he failed to see it as a complete story. Obviously he was not able to determine the main ideas.

Many readers are like my young movie-goer. They are sometimes too over-whelmed by the onslaught of images, vocabulary, and scenes throughout a text to remember that they need to continuously ask themselves "What is it about?" They need to figure out what the author thought was important. Teaching children to determine importance in the text, means that we need to teach them to be critical thinkers while they are reading. They need to pause frequently and think about their reading. They need to become savvy detectives, attending to important ideas and learning how to filter out the rest as possibly interesting but not important.

When we teach students to determine important information, they move from the simple tasks of determining *what* is important, to the more sophisticated skills of determining *why* something is important and providing evidence to support their opinion.

Summarizing a story into one main idea (see first sample above) is a challenging skill for some students; however I think this young reader says it best. After reading *Goldilocks and the Three Bears*, he decisively stated that the most important thing he learned was: "Never go into a bear's home"—an important life lesson for all!

The second sample provides students with the opportunity of describing and illustrating two things that they learned; in this case, from *All About Canadian Communities: Northern Communities*. This task works well for both fiction and non-fiction. Its open-endedness allows for a wide range complexities of responses.

The final task is intended for a more sophisticated reader. In this task, students again identify three main ideas from the text; however, they must be able to justify their selection. Extending their thinking further, students provide evidence from the text to support their thinking. They can provide a quote from the book, or they may choose to paraphrase another event in the book; in this case, *The White Horse Talisman* by Andrea Spalding. Examining students' reflections will give a good indication of their level of thinking about the book.

Determining Importance Task Descriptions: Fiction

The following task boxes aid students in identifying the most important information in a variety of texts. Students learn to record the main ideas in different ways, provide evidence from the text to support their thinking, and retell information using their own words.

DETERMINING IMPORTANCE: WHAT'S MOST IMPORTANT?

Using the graphic organizer, students record the one thing they think was most important to remember about the text. Students may include an illustration to support their ideas. Some readers might think about a specific element from the text (e.g., Billy was a bully), while others may identify a lesson learned from the story (e.g., Treat others the way you want to be treated).

DETERMINING IMPORTANCE: RETELL KEY IDEAS

This task is a natural extension of the previous one; students record more than one important idea from the text. Some students may include both themes from the text and specific information about the text. Sophisticated readers might make an extension to their thinking by providing the rationale for their selection. They may form connections between two ideas from the text; for example, they may determine that something that occurs early in the text is important, because it causes a later event to occur.

DETERMINING IMPORTANCE: SEQUENCING IDEAS (PRIMARY)

Breaking a story in to three major events will help students to begin retelling a text using sequencing words. In this task, students identify three events in the story and create an illustration to represent each. Under each illustration, they write one sentence to describe what happened. By combining the three ideas using the sequencing words (*first*, *then*, and *finally*), young readers have effectively created a sequenced summary of the text.

DETERMINING IMPORTANCE: SEQUENCING IDEAS (JUNIOR)

This task invites students to divide a text into three important events and describe them sequentially. The graphic organizer allows students to respond in creative ways. Some students may choose to respond using sentences to fully describe certain events; others may use illustrations supported by some writing. Some readers might include three events that are directly connected through cause and effect.

The reproducible boxes on pages 118–122 can be copied and placed into Reading 8-Boxes for students' use.

**Determining Importance
What's Most Important?**

What do you think is the most important thing to remember about the story?

**Determining Importance
Retell Key Ideas**

Retell the most important ideas from the text. You can include a picture to help explain your ideas.

**Determining Importance
Sequencing Ideas (primary)**

Create three pictures showing the three most important events in the story. Under each picture write one sentence to describe what it is showing.

**Determining Importance
Sequencing Ideas (junior)**

Describe three important events that happen in the book. Remember to use sequencing words like "first," "then," and "finally."

**Determining Importance
Beginning, Middle, End**

Retell the story with pictures and words.

Beginning

**Determining Importance
Three-Frame Comic Strip**

Using information from the book, retell the story by drawing a three-frame cartoon. Make sure your cartoon strip has a good beginning, middle, and ending.

**Determining Importance
Six-Frame Comic Strip**

Create a comic strip showing the most important events in the story. Under each frame, write one sentence to describe what it is showing.

**Determining Importance
Understanding Characters**

In what ways does knowing more about the characters help you to understand the story better?

**Determining Importance
Character Traits**

Describe three character traits of one character from the book. Provide evidence from the text that demonstrates each character trait.

**Determining Importance
Conflict and Resolution**

What was the main problem or conflict that the character(s) faced in the story?

DETERMINING IMPORTANCE: BEGINNING, MIDDLE, END

Students retell the story using pictures and words. They divide the text into the beginning, middle, and end, and illustrate and describe accordingly. Some students may choose to write one continuous passage, while others may divide their writing into paragraphs. By chunking their ideas into sections, they will be able to retell the most important ideas in a sequential manner.

DETERMINING IMPORTANCE: THREE-FRAME COMIC STRIP

Using this alternative form of media, students are able to retell the three main ideas (beginning, middle, and end) or three sequential ideas. Students enjoy creating humorous representations of the characters and including thought/speech bubbles to help clarify their drawings.

DETERMINING IMPORTANCE: SIX-FRAME COMIC STRIP

As in the previous task, students use the medium of a comic strip to retell the most important events in a story. They can use a variety of texts to help explain their drawings. Some students may use speech/thought bubbles, and others may include sentences under each frame to further clarify their thinking. Proficient readers who are reading longer books may choose to represent only a portion of the text with this task. They may be able to effectively summarize one chapter (or perhaps the climax of the story) using the six frames.

DETERMINING IMPORTANCE: UNDERSTANDING CHARACTERS

As readers strengthen their understanding of certain characters, it becomes easier for them to understand their motives and interpret their actions. In this task, students think about their knowledge of a character and describe how it helped them to better understand a portion of the story. This task may more effective toward the end of the book, as the character may have developed significantly throughout the text and the reader may have become much more familiar with the character. Students may need to make some inferences as they draw conclusions about the character and use this information to understand the story.

DETERMINING IMPORTANCE: CHARACTER TRAITS

In this task, readers select one character and identify three of his/her character traits. They provide evidence from the text to support each of the traits. Some students may include direct quotes; others may include an example from the text of a situation where the character demonstrated a specific trait; and others may explain how they came to a conclusion about a character based on an example from the text. Students often need to be reminded that a character trait is not a physical feature but a defining element of the character's personality.

DETERMINING IMPORTANCE: CONFLICT AND RESOLUTION

The conflict in the story is the main problem that the characters are faced with. In this task, students identify the conflict and describe the ways in which it was solved. Readers then evaluate the actions taken by the characters, and explain whether they agree or disagree with the solution. Some students may be able to make connections to previous personal experiences that can help them have a greater insight into the characters or the situation.

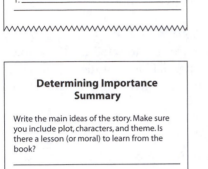

Determining Importance
Three Interesting Things

What are the three most interesting things you learned from reading the story? Tell why you think each one was interesting.

1. _____

Determining Importance
Summary

Write the main ideas of the story. Make sure you include plot, characters, and theme. Is there a lesson (or moral) to learn from the book?

_____

DETERMINING IMPORTANCE: THREE INTERESTING THINGS

In this task, students identify three interesting things they learned while reading the text and provide the rationale for their selection. Some students may refer to specific elements in the text, while others may see the text in a broader perspective and refer to underlying themes or lessons that may be prevalent throughout the text. It is interesting to see the differences in the depth of thinking that readers bring to this task. Some may be very literal in their interpretation of the text and others may provide a great deal of insight into the text.

DETERMINING IMPORTANCE: SUMMARY

Students are asked to summarize the main ideas of the story. They are reminded of the key elements of the story: characters, plot, setting, and theme. Readers use sequencing words to organize their thoughts, form well-developed paragraphs, and provide adequate evidence for their thinking. This open-response task allows teachers the opportunity to assess the ways in which students organize their writing to respond to a question requiring a multi-step answer. Stronger readers may include inferences and conclusions that they made while they were reading.

Determining Importance Task Descriptions: Non-Fiction

DETERMINING IMPORTANCE: KWL

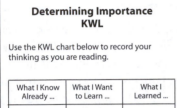

Determining Importance
KWL

Use the KWL chart below to record your thinking as you are reading.

What I Know Already ...	What I Want to Learn ...	What I Learned ...

A KWL chart helps students track their understanding of a topic as they continue to learn more about it. In the first column students list what they already know about a subject; in the second column they record things that they would like to learn; and finally, as they learn new things, they add these to the final column. This task should be used throughout the reading so that, as readers' knowledge changes, they are able to record their new learning.

DETERMINING IMPORTANCE: MAIN IDEA AND SUPPORTING DETAILS

Determining Importance
Main Idea and Supporting Details

Identify three main ideas from the text and find supporting details for each of the ideas.

Using a non-fiction text, students select three main ideas and supporting details for each. They may select the main ideas from one section of text or from sections throughout the text. This task leads nicely into a mini-lesson on paragraph writing or research skills. Students could use a similar organizer to arrange their own ideas to strengthen their personal writing.

DETERMINING IMPORTANCE: IMPORTANT IDEAS CHART

Determining Importance
Important Ideas Chart

Summarize three of the most important ideas in the book. Tell why you think each idea is important and provide evidence from the text to support your thinking.

Students identify and describe three important ideas that they learned from the text. It is possible in this task, as in the previous one, to see a range of insight into the texts. In this task, students are asked to justify their selections with a rationale (why did they think this was important) and support their idea with evidence from the text.

DETERMINING IMPORTANCE: FACT, EVIDENCE, OPINION

Determining Importance
Fact, Evidence, Opinion

Select three interesting facts you have learned while reading the book. For each, summarize the fact, provide evidence from the text, and give your opinion (what did you think when you learned this fact?).

In the first column of the table, students summarize three interesting facts that they learned while reading the book. In the second column, they provide the evidence from the text that supports their ideas. In the final column they give their opinion, what they thought when they initially read the fact, a response to the fact, or a personal connection that came to mind.

**Determining Importance
Fishbone**

Identify three main ideas and provide
supporting details for each.

**Determining Importance
Cause and Effect**

Choose three things that are explained in the
text. Describe how they are affected by
various factors.

**Determining Importance
Fact or Opinion**

An opinion is someone's personal
perspective on a subject. As you read through
the text, record examples of facts and
opinions.

**Determining Importance
Ranking Ladder**

Identify five facts from the book. Use the
ranking ladder to order these facts from least
important to most important.

DETERMINING IMPORTANCE: FISHBONE

Students use the fishbone graphic organizer to record three main ideas and supporting details for each. A main idea is written on the top branch of each section of the fishbone and supporting ideas are listed under each. Students need to be able to summarize effectively, in order to concisely record each main idea and supporting details.

DETERMINING IMPORTANCE: CAUSE AND EFFECT

When looking for connections between ideas within a text, it is often possible to link these ideas through cause and effect. Using this chart, students record three things that are explained in the text; they describe what happened and why it may have happened. Readers need to interpret the information carefully in order to accurately describe them using cause and effect.

DETERMINING IMPORTANCE: FACT AND OPINION

In non-fiction texts, many facts are presented in conjunction with various opinions. Critical readers need to be able to determine the difference between facts and opinions. In this task, students record examples of facts and opinions that are found throughout the text.

DETERMINING IMPORTANCE: RANKING LADDER

Students identify five facts from the text. They then use the ranking ladder to organize the ideas in order of importance from least important (at the bottom) to most important (at the top). By assigning a rank to each fact, students evaluate the information. Readers will develop critical thinking skills as they strive to order the facts appropriately. When conferencing with students, ask them to justify their choices in order to understand their thinking and ability to connect to the text.

Determining Importance
What's Most Important?

What do you think is the most important thing to remember about the story?

Determining Importance
Retell Key Ideas

Retell the most important ideas from the text. You can include a picture to help explain your ideas.

_____

_____

_____

_____

_____

Determining Importance
Sequencing Ideas (primary)

Create three pictures showing the three most important events in the story. Under each picture write one sentence to describe what it is.

First:

_____

Then:

_____

Finally:

_____

Determining Importance
Sequencing Ideas (junior)

Describe three important events that happen in the book. Remember to use sequencing words like "first," "then," and "finally."

Determining Importance
Beginning, Middle, End

Retell the story with pictures and words.

Beginning	
Middle	
End	

Determining Importance
Three-Frame Comic Strip

Using information from the book, retell the story by drawing a three-frame cartoon. Make sure your cartoon strip has a good beginning, middle, and ending.

Determining Importance
Six-Frame Comic Strip

Create a comic strip showing the most important events in the story. Under each frame, write one sentence to describe what it is showing.

Determining Importance
Understanding Characters

In what ways does knowing more about the characters help you to understand the story better?

_____
_____
_____
_____
_____
_____
_____
_____
_____

Determining Importance
Character Traits

Describe three character traits of one character from the book. Provide evidence from the text that demonstrates each character trait.

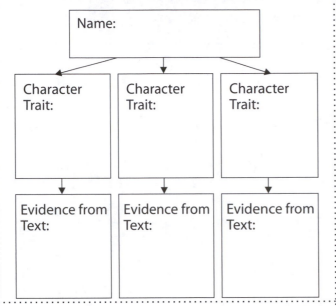

Name:

Character Trait:

Character Trait:

Character Trait:

Evidence from Text:

Evidence from Text:

Evidence from Text:

Determining Importance
Conflict and Resolution

What was the main problem or conflict that the character(s) faced in the story?

_____

_____

_____

How was the problem or conflict resolved?

_____

_____

_____

Do you agree with how the problem or conflict was resolved? Explain why you agree or disagree with the solution to the problem.

_____

Determining Importance
Three Interesting Things

What are the three most interesting things you learned from reading the story? Tell why you think each one was interesting.

1. _____

_____

This was interesting because:

_____

2. _____

_____

This was interesting because:

_____

3. _____

_____

This was interesting because:

Determining Importance
Summary

Write the main ideas of the story. Make sure you include plot, characters, and theme. Is there a lesson (or moral) to learn from the book?

_____

_____

_____

_____

_____

_____

_____

_____

_____

_____

Determining Importance
KWL

Use the KWL chart below to record your thinking as you are reading.

What I Know Already ...	What I Want to Learn ...	What I Learned ...

Determining Importance
Main Idea and Supporting Details

Identify three main ideas from the text and find supporting details for each of the ideas.

Main Idea:_____

Supporting Details:_____

_____

Main Idea:_____

Supporting Details:_____

_____

Main Idea:_____

Supporting Details:_____

_____

Determining Importance
Important Ideas Chart

Summarize three of the most important ideas in the book. Tell why you think each idea is important and provide evidence from the text to support your thinking.

Important Idea	Rationale	Evidence

Determining Importance
Fact, Evidence, Opinion

Select three interesting facts you have learned while reading the book. For each , summarize the fact, provide evidence from the text, and give your opinion (what did you think when you learned this fact?).

Fact	Evidence	Opinion

Determining Importance
Fishbone

Identify three main ideas and provide supporting details for each.

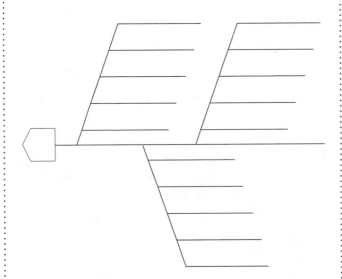

Determining Importance
Cause and Effect

Choose three things that are explained in the text. Describe how they are affected by various factors.

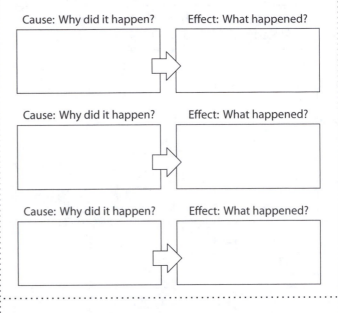

Cause: Why did it happen?　　Effect: What happened?

Cause: Why did it happen?　　Effect: What happened?

Cause: Why did it happen?　　Effect: What happened?

Determining Importance
Fact or Opinion

An opinion is someone's personal perspective on a subject. As you read through the text, record examples of facts and opinions.

Fact	Opinion

Determining Importance
Ranking Ladder

Identify five facts from the book. Use the ranking ladder to order these facts from least important to most important.

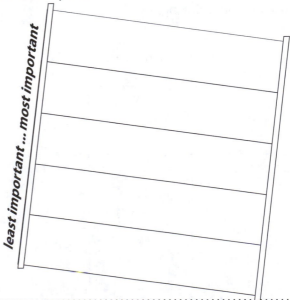

least important...most important

Rubric for Determining Importance

Skill	Level 1	Level 2	Level 3	Level 4
Reflect on learning and thinking while reading	Student rarely uses existing knowledge and information from the text to determine important ideas and rarely revises her/his thinking accordingly.	Student sometimes uses existing knowledge and information from the text to determine important ideas and may revise his/her thinking accordingly.	Student uses existing knowledge and information from the text to determine important ideas and revises his/her thinking accordingly.	Student thoughtfully uses existing knowledge and information from the text to determine important ideas and revises his/her thinking accordingly.
Identify important information, ideas, and supporting details in texts	Few key ideas and important information from the text are recorded.	Some of the key ideas and important information from the text are recorded.	Most of the key ideas and important information from the text are recorded.	All of the key ideas and important information from the text are recorded.
Sequence important information, ideas, and supporting details in texts	Few key ideas and important information from the text are recorded; may be sequenced incorrectly.	Some key ideas and important information from the text are sequenced correctly.	Most of the key ideas and important information from the text are sequenced correctly.	All of the key ideas and important information from the text are sequenced correctly.
Summarize important ideas	Few of the important ideas are included in a summary of the text.	Some of the important ideas are included in a summary of the text.	Most of the important ideas are included in a logical summary of the text.	All of the important ideas are included in a creative summary of the text.

Synthesizing

The "Hamburger" sample is on *Energy at the Airport*; the Summarizing task is on *The Withces* by Roald Dahl..

Once students are able to determine important ideas from a text, they will often share these ideas with others. When we retell or summarize something, we usually attach some personal interpretation to the text. By merging our thinking with the author's, we are able to share responses that are based both on the text and our personal experiences. Synthesizing is the process of combining the ideas in the text with one's own ideas to create something new and different. It is the evolution of our ideas as we progress through a text. As we read, we are thinking of ideas, making sense of the words, and generating thoughts of our own. When more information is added to our existing thought, we may broaden or alter our ideas. It is this self-reflection that defines synthesis. Not only are we thinking, but we are thinking about our thinking, reflecting on these thoughts, and reshaping them to include new information.

When teaching students about synthesizing, we need to help them recognize that thoughts evolve, change, and grow through time and experience.

Synthesizing tasks require students to think about the text in a different way; for example, asking them to consider the story from a point of view that may not have been presented in the text. This is sometimes challenging for young readers, as they mistake it for a chance to change major elements in the story. For example, in the familiar story The Three Little Pigs, they may say that if the Big Bad Wolf were telling the story he would have caught the little pigs and ate them for supper. What students often struggle to realize is that the events remain the same; the only thing that is different is the person who is telling the story.

In the first task below, students are asked to write a paragraph about a main idea that they have learned from the book. This is particularly well suited for non-fiction texts and provides a good opportunity to introduce students to research and report writing. Readers can select one main idea from the text, describe supporting details, and formulate a concluding sentence.

The "Hamburger" sample is on *Energy at the Airport*; the Summarizing task is on *The Withces* by Roald Dahl.

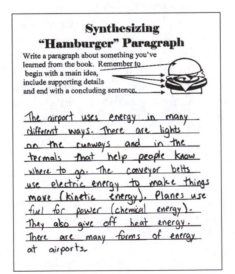

Synthesizing "Hamburger" Paragraph

Write a paragraph about something you've learned from the book. Remember to begin with a main idea, include supporting details and end with a concluding sentence.

The airport uses energy in many different ways. There are lights on the runways and in the termals that help people know where to go. The conveyor belts use electric energy to make things move (kinetic energy). Planes use fuel for power (chemical energy). They also give off heat energy. There are many forms of energy at airports.

Summarizing

Retell the story using your own words.

This book is all about bald, disgust, tooless, evil, female witches. Once, a child lived with his mother and father, but one day, the childs parents died from a car crash. The child lives with his grandma, and went to a hotel for the childs summer vacation. In the hotel the child found a whole bunch of witches. However the child gets caught and turns into a mice! The child (mice) and his grandma turn all the witches into mice by a secret potion named "Number 86 delayed mousemaker." Now the child and his grandma will try to get rid of every witches in the world!

The reproducible boxes on pages 127–129 can be copied and placed into Reading 8-Boxes for students' use.

The second sample task requires students to think of their book in its entirety. They need to create an effective summary that captures the essence of the book without giving away the ending. Students enjoy the challenge of finding just the right words to make their book seem enticing and exciting. They may have read a number of book summaries and are eager to take on the challenge themselves. When you are reviewing students' work, a task like this can be a good indicator of their understanding of the text and its elements (characters, setting, plot, theme, lesson, etc.)

Synthesizing Task Descriptions

SYNTHESIZING: LESSONS LEARNED

Students describe something learned from the book. Readers are able reflect on the most important information in the text and combine it with their own thinking to create a brief summary of the main idea or moral of the story. It is interesting to note which ideas students deem the most important once they have finished reading the book.

SYNTHESIZING: INTERESTING TEXT

Students use information from the text and their own experiences to explain why they found the book interesting. When presenting their opinions, students justify their thinking by combining their own ideas with ideas from the text. Students might present a range of ideas that they describe briefly, or they might expand on one idea in great detail.

SYNTHESIZING: SUMMARIZING

In this task, students retell the story using their own words. The open-ended nature of this task allows you the opportunity to assess students' understanding of the text. Some students may effectively sequence their ideas and form well-organized paragraphs, including main ideas and supporting details. Proficient readers include sequencing words and a complete description of the various elements of the text. Other students may even include personal opinions and conclusions that they made while reading.

SYNTHESIZING: CHARACTER'S PERSPECTIVE

Students consider ways in which the story would have been different had a different character been telling the story. Readers can think about different points of view that various characters may bring to one situation. You might need to remind students that the major elements in the story should remain the same; it is the the point of view that will be different.

SYNTHESIZING: ALTERNATIVE POINT OF VIEW

Considering a story from an alternative point of view often provides readers with a great deal of insight. In life, all stories have multiple points of view. This task encourages readers to think about the story from the perspective of a different character. Students need to recognize that the elements of the plot are not to be altered, but the way they are presented might be very different if told by a different character.

SYNTHESIZING: ALTERING CHARACTERS

In this task, students are invited to explore the possibility of altering one character and considering the effects that would have on the plot. Students describe the ways in which the story would differ should one character be changed in some way; for example, if the character was a girl instead of a boy, or was ten years older.

**Synthesizing
Lessons Learned**

Use your own words to describe something you learned from the book.

**Synthesizing
Interesting Text**

Using information from the text and your own experience, explain in sentences why this book is interesting.

**Synthesizing
Summarizing**

Retell the story using your own words.

**Synthesizing
Character's Perspectives**

How might the story be different if a different character was telling the story?

**Synthesizing
Alternative Point of View**

Retell the story from another character's point of view.

**Synthesizing
Altering Characters**

How would the story have been different if one of the characters were changed in some way (e.g., was a girl instead of a boy, or was ten years older)?

**Synthesizing
Altering Elements**

If you were the author, what would you have
changed in the book? Perhaps you might have
changed the ending or one of the characters
— how would the story have been different?

**Synthesizing
Altering Actions**

How do you think the story would change if a
character in the story made a different
decision or choice?

**Synthesizing
Audience Appeal**

How could you change the book to appeal to
a different or wider audience? _____
_____

**Synthesizing
PMI**

Think about an important decision a
character had to make. Complete the PMI
chart below. What are some Pluses (positive
things) about the decision? What are some

**Synthesizing
Back Cover**

Pretend you are the publisher. Your job is to
create an exciting summary to put at the back
of the book. It needs to tell what the story is
about, without giving too much away. What

**Synthesizing
"Hamburger" Paragraph**

Write a paragraph about something you've
learned from the book. Remember to
begin with a main idea, include
supporting details, and
end with a concluding sentence.

SYNTHESIZING: ALTERING ELEMENTS

The various elements of a text are so interconnected that changing one feature may have significant effects on the entire story. This task encourages students to consider different ways in which the author may have changed the story. Readers are to choose one possible change that the author may have made to the story (e.g., a different ending), and describe ways in which the story would have been different.

SYNTHESIZING: ALTERING ACTIONS

In this task, students consider the changes that may have resulted had one character acted in a different way when faced with an important decision. Readers describe the character's decision in the text and then think about the ways the story would have been different had they acted differently. Sometimes minor decisions may result in major differences in the outcomes of situations.

SYNTHESIZING: AUDIENCE APPEAL

This task invites students to consider the audience for whom the book was intended. Readers are asked to consider what changes could be made in order to make the book appeal to a different audience (perhaps younger or older). They might consider various biases or perspectives that are introduced through the book; they might also think about the author's word choice and use of images throughout the text. This is quite a challenging task, and is therefore better suited for proficient readers and critical thinkers.

SYNTHESIZING: PMI

The PMI chart asks students to consider the positive, negative, and interesting things about a decision made by one of the characters. Considering the different dimensions to a decision helps readers apply their knowledge of the characters and situation. Students consider the actions of the character prior to making the decision and the consequences that followed later.

SYNTHESIZING: BACK COVER

In this task, students think like a publisher and create an exciting synopsis to be placed on the back cover of the book. Students need to include enough information to describe what the story is about without giving too much away. Students enjoy the challenge of making their book seem exciting and inviting.

SYNTHESIZING: "HAMBURGER" PARAGRAPH

This task uses the familiar hamburger graphic to assist students in writing a complete paragraph about something they have learned by reading the text. They begin with a main idea, provide supporting details, and end with a concluding sentence.

Synthesizing
Lessons Learned

Use your own words to describe something you learned from the book.

_____

_____

_____

_____

_____

Draw a picture to help explain your thinking:

Synthesizing
Interesting Text

Using information from the text and your own experience, explain in sentences why this book is interesting.

_____

_____

_____

_____

_____

_____

_____

_____

_____

_____

_____

Synthesizing
Summarizing

Retell the story using your own words.

_____

_____

_____

_____

_____

_____

_____

_____

_____

_____

Synthesizing
Character's Perspectives

How might the story be different if a different character was telling the story?

Synthesizing
Alternative Point of View

Retell the story from another character's point of
view.

_____

_____

_____

_____

_____

_____

_____

_____

Synthesizing
Altering Characters

How would the story have been different if one of
the characters were changed in some way (e.g.,
was a girl instead of a boy, was ten years older)?

_____

_____

_____

_____

_____

_____

_____

_____

Synthesizing
Altering Elements

If you were the author, what would you have
changed in the book? Perhaps you might have
changed the ending or one of the characters—
how would the story have been different?

_____

_____

_____

_____

_____

_____

_____

Synthesizing
Altering Actions

How do you think the story would change if a
character in the story made a different decision or
choice?

Character's decision or choice in the text:

_____

_____

_____

How do you think the story would change if a
character in the story made a different decision or
choice?

_____

_____

_____

Synthesizing
Audience Appeal

How could you change the book to appeal to a different or wider audience?

_____

_____

_____

_____

_____

_____

_____

_____

Synthesizing
PMI

Think about an important decision a character had to make. Complete the PMI chart below. What are some Pluses (positive things) about the decision? What are some Minuses (negative things) about the decision? Some Interesting Things that you discovered?

Plus (+)	Minus (−)	Interesting Things

Synthesizing
Back Cover

Pretend you are the publisher. Your job is to create an exciting summary to put at the back of the book. It needs to tell what the story is about, without giving too much away. What would you say?

_____

_____

_____

_____

_____

_____

_____

Synthesizing
"Hamburger" Paragraph

Write a paragraph about something you've learned from the book. Remember to begin with a main idea, include supporting details, and end with a concluding sentence.

_____

_____

_____

_____

_____

_____

_____

_____

Rubric for Synthesizing

Skill	Level 1	Level 2	Level 3	Level 4
Summarize the main ideas of a text	Summary may omit the main ideas or demonstrate limited understanding of the text.	Main ideas of the text are somewhat summarized.	Main ideas of the text are clearly summarized.	Main ideas of the text are clearly summarized; student's own thoughts/ideas/opinions are added to the summary.
Identify ways in which thoughts have developed while reading a text	Student identifies few ideas generated while reading the text; finds it challenging to describe ways in which his/her thinking has changed.	Student identifies some ideas generated while reading the text; is beginning to describe ways in which his/her thinking has changed.	Student identifies a number of different ideas generated while reading the text; is able to describe ways in which his/her thinking has changed.	Student clearly identifies a number of different ideas generated while reading the text; is able to consistently describe ways in which his/her thinking has changed.
Combine important ideas from the text with own thinking to form a greater understanding of the text	Ideas may be copied from the text and/or not combined with the student's own thinking; student demonstrates a limited understanding of the text.	Important ideas from the text are somewhat combined with the student's own thinking; student demonstrates a satisfactory understanding of the text.	Important ideas from the text are combined with the student's own thinking; student demonstrates a good understanding of the text.	Many important ideas from the text are creatively combined with the student's own thinking; student demonstrates a thorough understanding of the text.
Examine the choices made by the author and consider alternatives	Student finds it challenging to consider any ways that the text would have been different had major elements of the story been altered.	Student is able to consider simple ways that the text would have been different had major elements of the story been altered.	Student is able to consider a variety of ways that the text would have been different had major elements of the story been altered.	Student is able to consider a variety of ways that the text would have been different had major elements of the story been altered; creatively describes the effects that these changes would have had on the outcome of the book.

7 Reading 8-Boxes in the Classroom

Consider the following scenario: The language block is well in swing. The teacher has just completed a read-aloud, during which she reinforced the reading strategy of *making connections*. This has been the instructional focus for many of the large- and small-group lessons in the past two weeks. Many students are now quite familiar with the range of connections that they might make while reading and are comfortable with the associated terminology.

After a few minutes, the teacher calls a group of students to the round table for a guided reading lesson. In the meantime, the remainder of the class is working on their independent reading and Reading 8-Boxes. They are nearing the end of this set of 8-Boxes; some students have completed all eight tasks, while others are putting the final touches on the last two task boxes to be handed in the next day.

Some students return excitedly from the library, three holding fiction novels and the fourth thrilled about his new discovery of the wonders of volcanoes. They rush to a bulletin board that contains five pocket folders. Each pocket folder contains a different set of Reading 8-Boxes. As the students independently peruse the 8-Boxes, they notice that each contains a similar Connecting task in the lower right corner. They begin to compare and contrast the requirements of each of the different 8-Boxes. The student with the volcano book discovers that he can select from two different non-fiction Reading 8-Boxes and selects one that provides him opportunities to question and visualize (these reading strategies being his strength). The remaining students have a choice of three fiction 8-Boxes: one selects a Reading 8-Box that contains a Determining Importance box and a favorite Word Skills activity. The last two students share a brief discussion about a recent conference in which their teacher reminded them both that they should revisit the strategy of Inferring. Finally they decide to select the same Reading 8-Box, one that includes one task box on Inferring and a Text Element task that focuses on plot development.

> By choosing from a carefully considered selection of Reading 8-Boxes, students can independently select a focus for their continued learning in the absence of the teacher, but with the teacher's guidance.

While the teacher has continued with the guided reading lesson, the students have facilitated their own learning. By setting stage for effective learning to occur, the teacher has guided the students in their self-directed learning.

Finding the Right Combination

The task boxes in this book can be combined to form countless combinations of sets of Reading 8-Boxes. Many of the tasks are very versatile and can easily be

Use the template on pages 138–139 to arrange photocopied task boxes into a Reading 8-Box for reproducing.

When selecting tasks to include on a Reading 8-Box, the following are important to consider:

• the skills being intentionally targeted
• the range of knowledge and experiences of the students
• the genre of the texts.

used with students from a range of grades and abilities, as well as working with a variety of texts, including fiction and non-fiction.

It is best for students if all Reading 8-Boxes follow a similar format. That way, students quickly adjust to the differing requirements of each task, and are familiar with the overall expectations. The typical Reading 8-Box includes one task that focuses on each of the areas of language development (text selection, text elements, word skills, and the taxonomy of thinking) and four that target reading comprehension strategies.

In a classroom, at any given time, students are probably reading varying types of books at a range of levels. It is not possible to construct Reading 8-Boxes for each and every student based on their individual needs and texts. Therefore, it is best to assist students in choosing appropriate Reading 8-Boxes from a selection available in the class. Initially, students may find it easier if everyone works on the same set of Reading 8-Boxes, as they can seek advice from their peers and assist each other, while still maintaining their independence. As students become more familiar with the requirements of Reading 8-Boxes, they will desire more control over their learning, and selection of the Reading 8-Box will become an important component of their self-directed learning. Creating a number of Reading 8-Boxes and having them available for students to choose from will enable learners to feel truly independent.

When assembling Reading 8-Boxes, consider the following:

1. Fiction and Non-Fiction
   Students may be reading a range of genres of books at any given time. Therefore, it is important to ensure either that the tasks are suitable for both fiction and non-fiction, or that some choice is available to students. It may be possible to have as few as two Reading 8-Boxes or as many as five or six.

2. Recent Classroom Instruction
   As the year progresses, the focus for reading instruction changes. Many teachers choose to address different reading strategies in greater depth at various times throughout the year. When a specific reading strategy has been the focus for instruction (large-group or guided reading), it should be included in the next set of Reading 8-Boxes, to provide students guided practice with this strategy and to build their competencies.

3. Individual Areas for Growth
   Through conferencing with students, guided reading, and the assessment of student work, teachers will note individual students' areas for continued growth. When students are made aware of these areas for further development, they are able to independently support this progress by selecting Reading 8-Boxes that include tasks that target their needs. When creating sets of 8-Boxes, take into account recent conferences with students and the specific areas of growth that were noted. It is not possible to include 30 different areas for growth on a Reading 8-Box that contains only eight tasks, so be selective and focused in directing students. It may be possible to see obvious trends and to group students accordingly.

4. Variety of Task Types
   The large selection of individual task boxes was designed to provide as many different learning experiences and to allow as many different forms of responses as possible. There are open-response opportunities, graphic organizers, and open-ended tasks for students to demonstrate their think-

ing in many ways. When assembling Reading 8-Boxes, it is important to maintain variety in the nature of the tasks. There should be some tasks in which the students write a complete answer using sentences, and also some opportunities to express themselves creatively (either with graphic organizers or drawings). Learning is much more purposeful and enjoyable when the tasks are varied.

Assembling the Reading 8-Boxes

Begin by selecting **one** task from each language area:

- My Reading
- Text Elements
- Word Skills
- Taxonomy of Thinking

Next, select **four** different comprehension strategies from the eight reading strategies:

- Monitoring Understanding
- Connecting
- Questioning
- Visualizing
- Inferring
- Predicting
- Determining Importance
- Synthesizing

Put together, the eight task boxes will create a unique Reading 8-Box that will directly support classroom instruction that has taken place.

The physical assembly of a Reading 8-Box is quite simple. Use a copy of the template on pages 138–139, or fold a large sheet of paper (11" x 17") into eight equal parts. Using photocopies of the reproducible task boxes that you have cut apart into separate boxes, glue one task box into each of the eight parts. Once all eight task boxes are in place, photocopy the completed 8-Box for the students to use.

Teaching One Box at a Time

Teaching students any new skill requires us to think of it in its most rudimentary components. Learning to use the task boxes is analogous to learning to ride a bike. First, one must know what a bike looks like, where to sit, and the purpose of the vehicle. Second, a young child needs to try out the bike with lots of supports in place. Usually, this entails a trip to the local hardware store to purchase and attach a pair of training wheels. Finally, when the child has had sufficient practice (and usually seen her friends with a two-wheeler), we remove the training wheels and let her attempt to ride independently. When working with task boxes, the first step, awareness of task boxes, can be achieved through modeling. During read-aloud times, teachers can help students understand the purpose of

Find reproducible task boxes on the following pages:

- My Reading: page 28
- Text Elements: pages 36–40
- Word Skills: pages 47–51
- Taxonomy of Thinking: pages 60–64, 67–69
- Monitoring Understanding: pages 74–75
- Connecting: pages 82–85
- Questioning: pages 91–94
- Visualizing: pages 99–101
- Inferring: pages 106–107
- Predicting: page 111
- Determining Importance: pages 118–122
- Synthesizing: pages 127–129

Building task boxes into an already existing language program should not require alterations to the structure of the program. Task boxes are not add-ons, but are designed to be integrated into the main components of the program, in order to lead to a more focused independent reading time.

task boxes, how they are used, and what expectations the teacher has associated with them. Secondly, guided practice can easily be built into small-group instruction times, such as those for guided reading. This gives students time to try out new learning with the teacher's support and structure. Finally comes independence: the ultimate goal of every instructional tool. Leading our students to independence provides them with time to practice and enjoy their new skills.

The components of a balanced reading program should not be independent of each other; instead instruction should flow seamlessly between the various elements in order to continually strengthen and reinforce instruction.

Model through Read-Aloud

When introducing students to a new reading concept or strategy, beginning with a read-aloud allows students to observe a reader in action. Select one individual task to share with students prior to reading aloud. This sharing will allow them to focus their listening to the parts of the text that will be needed in order to successfully complete that activity. If possible, make an enlarged copy of the individual task box on a piece of 11" x 17" paper, or reproduce it on chart paper so that it is easily seen by all students. During the reading, take time to discuss the task and how the task box can be used to record thinking while reading. Consider allowing time for students to share their thinking with elbow-partners while reading aloud. This reduces the fear of risk-taking and allows all students opportunities to "try it out" with someone beside them. Opportunities for these interactive breaks while reading aloud helps students validate their thinking by knowing that their ideas have been heard. It also allows for students to learn from their peers. Consider taking more interactive breaks instead of asking for students to raise their hands and selecting one student's voice to speak for everyone.

By modeling how to use the Thinking Box effectively to record students' thinking, the students will become comfortable with the task, and aware of the teacher's expectations.

Try Out with Guided Reading

After introducing students to a new concept or strategy through modeling and read-aloud, reintroduce the skill through guided reading. This does not necessarily mean that the same task needs to be re-taught. Consider a task box that may target a similar skill through a different task. Teachers need to consider the different needs of their learners in order to determine the level of practice necessary in order to build their competency. Younger children would be more comfortable with seeing a familiar task box revisited, while older students will be ready to move onto a new challenge. Discussing the task boxes through guided reading allows for students to practice skills in a way that is still supported by the teacher.

Supporting students' learning through guided practice helps to scaffold their learning and there is a gradual release of responsibility from the teacher to the individual student.

Gradual Release of Responsibility

The final component of reading skill acquisition is guided practice. Younger students will need to have familiar task boxes for their independent reading; older students may need only a mini-lesson on the target expectations and requirements for new task. Younger students may wish to start with individual boxes and gradually add to their repertoire, while older students may feel comfortable with a wider selection of tasks. Students need time to experiment, explore, and integrate new learning into their reading. Independent reading time is when students are able to internalize and apply their new reading skills. By scaffolding their independent reading through task boxes, we provide students with a greater opportunity to practice specific strategies, and we are more able to monitor their progress.

It was December, and I was teaching a mini-lesson to my class. Firmly in the routine, I said, "Now, turn to your elbow-partner and share your thinking about…" Suddenly, one student's eyes lit up as if a light bulb had gone off inside his head. Unable to contain his ideas, he jumped up and shouted: "OH, I GET IT! Every time you teach us something new, first you show us how to do it, then we do it with a partner, then you make us do it on our own!" I smiled and thought to myself: *It took you **three months** to figure that out? It took me **eleven years**.*

Putting It All Together

Assembled Reading 8-Boxes are organized to provide students with multiple opportunities for learning. Each set of eight task boxes includes four tasks that focus on reading comprehension strategies and one task on each of the following: text selection, word skills, text elements, and the taxonomy of thinking.

When students become more comfortable with the various requirements of each task, it becomes possible to combine them into sets that will help them demonstrate their understanding of texts through a variety of tasks. If Reading 8-Boxes are introduced early in the year, by mid-year it is possible to have a range of 8-Boxes that students are comfortable with.

Teachers may choose to have all students working on the same Reading 8-Boxes as a way of reinforcing large-group instruction, or students within one class may be working on a variety of 8-Boxes that specifically address their needs and areas for growth. The flexibility and range of instructional level allows teachers to provide much-needed diversified instruction for all students. As we get to know our students' strengths and needs through small-group instruction, we become much more able to guide their independent reading choices and identify areas for their continued growth.

For example, a teacher may recognize the need for one group of students to strengthen their skills at making connections. This can be an instructional focus during small-group instruction, and then students have the opportunity to choose from two or three different sets of 8-Boxes for their independent reading—all include one task aimed at strengthening their connecting skills. The students maintain their choice, and the teacher is able to effectively direct the students' learning. A variety of tasks on the same set of Reading 8-Boxes provides students the opportunity to demonstrate their competencies in other areas and meet with greater success.

It is important that each Reading 8-Box include a variety of task styles. The open-ended style of graphic organizers makes it easy for student to represent their thinking in abstract, random ways, whereas the open-response tasks provide opportunities for students to formulate complete answers, express their ideas in full thoughts, and provide evidence from the text. It is important both to consider our students' thought processes while evaluating their 8-Boxes and to provide them with the opportunity to respond in complete answers.

Consider having a bulletin board with pocket folders containing copies of a number of different Reading 8-Boxes. With a little direction from the teacher, students can independently select both their texts for reading and the Reading 8-Boxes with task boxes they are eager to fill out—true independence!

A complete Reading 8-Box should include tasks from a range of styles. The task boxes give students the opportunity to respond in a variety of ways. Some tasks are intended to strengthen students' ability to create open-response answers, whereas others use graphic organizers as a tool to organize students' thinking.

Although the number of possible combinations of unique and engaging Reading 8-Boxes is limitless, the charts found in the Appendix: Suggested Reading 8-Boxes on pages 141–148 may provide some useful guidelines for getting started. The individual tasks are combined into Reading 8-Box descriptions that each target a range of skills. The series of Reading-8-Box descriptions includes a progression of skills for both fiction and non-fiction texts. The 8-Boxes described early in the Appendix would be suitable for younger readers, whereas the later tasks allow proficient readers more opportunities to critically examine their books. These suggestions are not intended to limit the teacher's creativity; however, they may serve as a good starting point to creating a range of Reading 8-Boxes.

Using Reading 8-Boxes

How often should students complete Reading 8-Boxes, and how many? How can you make sure that they are finishing the tasks? When will you review your students' progress in their independent reading? The individual dynamics of each class must be taken into account when using Reading 8-Boxes. Consider the following options:

Option 1. Students are required to bring their Reading 8-Boxes when they meet with the teacher for guided reading. Upon quick review, the teacher can provide immediate feedback on the progress of individual students. The students' work may serve as a focus for a mini-lesson for further learning. This schedule provides a great opportunity to streamline assessment opportunities, as it is quite easy and efficient to evaluate a few 8-Boxes at once, rather than an entire class set. By taking a few minutes within the context of guided reading lessons, students can receive immediate feedback on their work, teachers can have a solid foundation for further instruction, and the efficiency of this ensures that the much dreaded "marking bin" remains empty.

Option 2. Students have an assigned day each week (e.g., Monday) for the completion of a set number of tasks (e.g., two boxes) in their Reading 8-Boxes. With this pre-established schedule, students can work at their own pace to read and respond. This ensures that the Reading 8-Box activities do not dominate their reading time, but serve as a tool to assess and guide independent reading appropriately. The expectation that they will complete two or three tasks a week provides students with adequate time to read, think, and complete their work.

Remember, the goal of the tasks in the Reading 8-Box is to support students' reading. It is important that teachers monitor the amount of time that students are spending reading and ensure that students are spending the majority of that time meaningfully engaged with their books.

With the amount of flexibility and independence that task boxes introduce into students' reading time, it is important to make sure that students persevere with all assigned tasks on an Reading 8-Box. Some students may be tempted to complete a few favorite tasks, then abandon the Reading 8-Box and begin a new one… only to complete their favorite tasks again. Students must complete all the assigned tasks to ensure that they are practicing a range of skills with their reading.

You might find it helpful to develop your own system to monitor students' completion of Reading 8-Boxes.

The Circle of Instruction

Introduction
Introduce, model, and teach individual tasks and Reading 8-Boxes.

Assessment and Evaluation
Evaluate responses on Reading 8-Boxes to determine student needs and to drive further instruction.

Application and Practice
Time to independently read self-selected texts, think about and apply new skills, and respond using Reading 8-Boxes.

This diagram illustrates the direct connection between the cycle of instruction and the guided practice provided by Reading 8-Boxes, showing the interdependence of Instruction, Application, and Assessment. Rather than falling in a sequential list, these instructional elements are more accurately illustrated as a circle, where each component is dependent on the others and instruction can flow between these parts.

Instruction helps students to develop new skills. Following this, students need time to apply and practice new skills that they have learned. The teacher should assess the work that the student has completed in order to determine his understanding of this new skill. This in turn will drive further instruction.

Teachers can use Reading 8-Boxes as a tool to directly reinforce skills that have been taught through instruction (large- or small-group). Reading 8-Boxes provide students with opportunities to try out new learning with their independent reading. Students are able to read a variety of texts, and have the opportunity to respond in a number of ways to strengthen their understanding. Regularly evaluating students' thinking about their reading by responding to their Reading 8-Boxes, teachers can determine areas for further instruction or effective groupings for guided reading.

My Reading

Text Elements

Reading Strategy

Reading Strategy

Word Skills

Taxonomy of Thinking

Reading Strategy

Reading Strategy

Appendix: Suggested Reading 8-Boxes

Fiction: Primary Grades

My Reading	Text Element *Setting: Picture and Sentence* Draw and describe the setting	Word Skills *Three Words and Pictures* Write and illustrate new words	Taxonomy of Thinking *Remembering: What's Happening?* Describe the most exciting part
Reading Strategy *Determining Importance: Sequencing Ideas (primary)* Illustrate and describe important events	**Reading Strategy** *Connecting to Personal Experiences* Text-to-self connection	**Reading Strategy** *Questioning: Using Prompts* Questions during reading	**Reading Strategy** *Visualizing a Character* Visualize character using words and pictures

My Reading	Text Element *Title* Relating the title to the text	Word Skills *Six Words and Pictures* Write and illustrate new words	Taxonomy of Thinking *Understanding: What's The Problem?* Identify problem and solution in story
Reading Strategy *Determining Importance: What's Most Important?* Identify main idea	**Reading Strategy** *Predicting at the Climax* Form prediction about climax of story	**Reading Strategy** *Visualizing a Favorite Character* Draw and describe favorite character	**Reading Strategy** *Inferring a Character's Feelings* Determining character's feelings and providing evidence

My Reading	Text Element *Plot: Sequencing Ideas* Sequencing three main ideas	Word Skills *Adjectives* Identifying adjectives from the text	Taxonomy of Thinking *Evaluating: Fairness* Form a judgment about the treatment of a character
Reading Strategy *Visualizing with Sight and Sound* Using senses (sight and sound) to describe text	**Reading Strategy** *Questioning for Understanding* Asking questions to monitor comprehension while reading	**Reading Strategy** *Inferring from a Character's Actions* Using character's actions to determine character's feelings	**Reading Strategy** *Connecting to Another Book* Text-to-text: Find similarities with another book

My Reading	Text Element *Characters: Who's Who?* Identify and describe important characters in text	Word Skills *Initial Sound* Identify words with the same initial sound	Taxonomy of Thinking *Applying: Lessons to Learn* Determine the main idea and purpose of the story
Reading Strategy *Visualizing a Specific Event* Create an image of a specific event in the book.	**Reading Strategy** *Questioning: Ravin' Reporter* Formulate questions for one character and create appropriate responses.	**Reading Strategy** *Determining Importance: Beginning, Middle, End* Retell picture with words and pictures (beginning, middle, end)	**Reading Strategy** *Monitoring Understanding: Strategies for Repairing Comprehension* Identify and strategies for monitoring comprehension

My Reading	Text Element *Title Choice* Matching the title to the text	Word Skills *Word Search* Identifying new vocabulary	Taxonomy of Thinking *Analyzing: Fiction Facts* Identify fictional elements in the story
Reading Strategy *Connecting to a Specific Character* Text-to-Self: Identify similarities between reader and a character from the text	**Reading Strategy** *Inferring: Character's Emotions* Provide examples of when a character displayed different emotions	**Reading Strategy** *Determining Importance: Character Traits* Identify character traits for one character and provide evidence from the text	**Reading Strategy** *Synthesizing: Altering Actions* Examining the choices made by a character and determining the outcome had they acted differently

My Reading	Text Element *Character Development (Primary)* Examine the changes in a character throughout the text	Word Skills *Verbs in Action* Identify and illustrate verbs from the text	Taxonomy of Thinking *Evaluating: Interesting Part* Draw and write about the most interesting part of the text
Reading Strategy *Connecting: Using a Venn Diagram* Text-to-text: Use a Venn Diagram to identify similarities and differences between two texts	**Reading Strategy** *Questioning the Characters or Author* Formulate questions for the author or characters in the text	**Reading Strategy** *Synthesizing: Alternative Point of View* Retell the story from an alternative perspective	**Reading Strategy** *Monitoring Understanding: Using a Checklist* Identify and evaluate strategies for monitoring comprehension

My Reading	Text Element	Word Skills	Taxonomy of Thinking
	Plot: Sequencing Ideas Sequencing three main ideas	*Nouns* Identify nouns from the text and categorize as people, places, or things	*Evaluating: Admirable Character Traits* Identify and describe admirable traits about the main character
Reading Strategy *Determining Importance: Understanding Characters* Developing a deeper understanding of the text through knowledge of characters	**Reading Strategy** *Questioning: Just One Question* Record the most important question that the reader would like answered. Justify their thinking.	**Reading Strategy** *Synthesizing: Altering Characters* Consider the effects of various character's characteristics on the outcome of the story	**Reading Strategy** *Monitoring Understanding: Word Attack and Comprehension* Evaluating and describing strategies for maintaining and repairing comprehension

My Reading	Text Element	Word Skills	Taxonomy of Thinking
	Fact or Fiction? Identify elements of the story that indicate it is fictional or true	*Guess and Check* Identify new vocabulary and confirm meaning using a dictionary	*Analyzing: Ordering Important Events* Evaluate and rank three important/exciting events from the text
Reading Strategy *Predicting: Using Early Clues* Use evidence from the text to formulate predictions	**Reading Strategy** *Connecting Through Similar Experiences* Text-to-self: Identify and describe similar experiences between the reader and the text	**Reading Strategy** *Questioning Using A Web* Create a web of questions	**Reading Strategy** *Monitoring Understanding: Evaluating Text* Evaluate and explain the difficulty level of the text

Fiction: Junior Grades

My Reading	Text Element	Word Skills	Taxonomy of Thinking
	Plot: Chain of Events Identify and describe sequence of events	*Synonyms and Antonyms* Use a thesaurus to find synonyms and antonyms for new vocabulary from text	*Evaluating: "I Disagree!"* Evaluate the actions of a character. Provide alternate options.
Reading Strategy *Connecting to a Character Through a Similar Experience* Text-to-self: Identify similarities between reader's experiences and problem in text	**Reading Strategy** *Inferring: Letter in Role* Write in role as one of the characters summarizing events and making predictions	**Reading Strategy** *Determining Importance: Conflict and Resolution* Identify conflict and resolution in text. Evaluate resolution of the conflict.	**Reading Strategy** *Synthesizing: PMI* Create PMI chart for one character in the text

My Reading	Text Element *Story Map* Complete a story map including Characters, Setting, and Plot (beginning, middle, and end)	Word Skills *Word Collector* Record new, interesting, or unfamiliar vocabulary	Taxonomy of Thinking *Creating: Alternative Solution* Find similarities and differences between two characters in the text
Reading Strategy *Determining Importance: Three-Frame Comic Strip* Using a three-frame comic strip, retell the story in sequence	**Reading Strategy** *Questioning and Looking for Answers* Record questions that aided with comprehension, and explain how the answers were found	**Reading Strategy** *Visualizing with Sight, Sound, and Smell* Use senses (sight, smell, sound) to visualize the text	**Reading Strategy** *Synthesizing: Character's Perspective* Consider ways in which the story would have been altered if told from a different perspective

My Reading	Text Element *Cover Information* Use information on the front and back cover to formulate predictions	Word Skills *Adjectives, Verbs, and Nouns* Identify and record adjectives, nouns, and verbs from the text	Taxonomy of Thinking *Creating: Alternative Actions* Reflecting on the decisions made by the main character
Reading Strategy *Determining Importance: Three Interesting Things* Identify and explain interesting ideas from the text	**Reading Strategy** *Predicting: Monitoring Predictions* Make predictions and determine whether they were correct or not	**Reading Strategy** *Connecting in a Variety of Ways* Text-to-self: Describe personal connections to the text (characters, setting, experiences, etc.)	**Reading Strategy** *Monitoring Understanding Using Prompts* Monitoring, repairing, and reflecting on comprehension of text

My Reading	Text Element *Character Development (Junior)* Examine the changes in a character throughout the text	Word Skills *Word Choice* Identify author's word choice to create vivid imagery	Taxonomy of Thinking *Remembering: Character Identification* Identify and describe characters from the text
Reading Strategy *Synthesizing: Summarizing* Retell the story	**Reading Strategy** *Connecting to Understand a Character's Actions* Text-to-self: Understanding a character's actions through similar personal experiences	**Reading Strategy** *Inferring a Character's Thoughts* Using a character's words and actions to infer their thoughts	**Reading Strategy** *Visualizing: Create a Magazine Advertisement* Use an alternate form of media (magazine advertisement) to promote the text

My Reading	Text Element *Setting: Picture and Evidence* Identify the setting of the story and provide supporting evidence (a quote) from the text	Word Skills *Instead of "Said"* Record words to replace the word "said"	Taxonomy of Thinking *Applying: Plan of Action* Using evidence from the text, formulate a plan of action for one character
Reading Strategy *Synthesizing: Back Cover* Create a new caption (summary) for the back cover of the book	**Reading Strategy** *Inferring: In a Character's Shoes* Analyzing the emotions and actions of the main character	**Reading Strategy** *Questioning Various Characters* Formulate questions for a number of characters in the story	**Reading Strategy** *Visualizing: Using all Five Senses* Use senses (sight, sound, smell, touch, and taste) to describe the text

My Reading	Text Element *Character Profile* Create a profile for one character	Word Skills *Adverbs* Identify verbs and adverbs throughout the text	Taxonomy of Thinking *Remembering: The 5 W's* General understanding of text (Who? What? When? Where? Why?)
Reading Strategy *Questioning: Before, During, and After* Record questions before, during and after reading. Search text for answers.	**Reading Strategy** *Connecting Using a Web* Use a graphic organizer (Web) to record reader's connections to the text	**Reading Strategy** *Determining Importance: Sequencing Ideas (junior)* Identify, describe, and sequence important events from the text	**Reading Strategy** *Synthesizing: Altering Elements* Consider ways in which the author may have changed the story (e.g., alternate ending)

My Reading	Text Element *Character Sketch* Create a character sketch for one character from the text	Word Skills *Adjectives and Adverbs* Record adjectives and adverbs from the text	Taxonomy of Thinking *Analyzing: Who's Most Important?* Judge the importance of various characters to the plot
Reading Strategy *Determining Importance: Six-Frame Comic Strip* Use an alternate form of media (comic strip) to summarize the important ideas	**Reading Strategy** *Inferring: Offering Advice* Provide advice to a character based on personal experiences	**Reading Strategy** *Questioning Recording and Reflecting on Questions* Record a variety of questions	**Reading Strategy** *Predicting Using Evidence* Record predictions made throughout the book, and provide supporting evidence from the text

My Reading	Text Element *Character Webs* Use a graphic organizer (web) to identify character traits for two characters. Provide evidence from the text	Word Skills *Using the Dictionary and Thesaurus* Select new/interesting vocabulary from the text. Use a dictionary and thesaurus to find the definition, and synonym.	Taxonomy of Thinking *Understanding: Summarizing Important Parts* Retell the most important part of the story
Reading Strategy *Determining Importance: Important Ideas Chart* Identify key ideas from the text and justify thinking with a rational and evidence from the text	Reading Strategy *Inferring: Lessons Learned* Describe lessons learned from the story and justify thinking with evidence from the text	Reading Strategy *Connecting to Specific Text* Record personal connections made while reading	Reading Strategy *Questioning: Letter to the Author* Write a letter to the author expressing questions pertaining to the text

My Reading	Text Element *Plot Graph* Use a graphic organizer (graph) to record the plot development throughout the text	Word Skills *Word Choice* Identify author's word choice to create vivid imagery	Taxonomy of Thinking *Creating: Who's Like You?* Explain personal connections to characters from the text
Reading Strategy *Determining Importance: Summary* Describe main ideas from the text (plot, characters, theme, etc.)	Reading Strategy *Visualizing: Celebrity Characters* Use images from an alternate form of media (celebrities) to strengthen mental images from the text	Reading Strategy *Connecting Using a Venn Diagram for a Variety of Connections* Use a graphic organizer (Venn Diagram) to record connections to the text	Reading Strategy *Synthesizing: Audience Appeal* Describe ways in which the book can be altered to appeal to a different audience

Non-Fiction: Primary Grades

My Reading	Text Element *Titles, Labels, Pictures* Identifying titles, labels, and pictures	Word Skills *Alphabetical Order* Identify new vocabulary and sort in alphabetical order	Taxonomy of Thinking *Evaluating: Favorite Part* Select and justify reader's favorite part
Reading Strategy *Synthesizing: Interesting Text* Use information from the text and personal experiences to explain how the text is interesting	Reading Strategy *Visualizing: Looks Like, Sounds Like, Feels Like* Select a main idea from the text and describe what it looks like, sounds like, and feels like	Reading Strategy *Determining Importance: Retell Key Ideas* Retell, with pictures and words, important ideas from the text	Reading Strategy *Monitoring Understanding: Favorite Fix-Ups* Explain strategies for monitoring and repairing comprehension

My Reading	Text Element	Word Skills	Taxonomy of Thinking
	Strengthening Understanding (primary) Explain how text elements (table of contents, index and illustrations) strengthen understanding	*Three Words and Pictures* Write and illustrate new words	*Understanding: Three Main Ideas* Describe three main ideas from the text
Reading Strategy *Determining Importance: KWL* Use graphic organizer (KWL chart) to record thinking as reading.	**Reading Strategy** *Questioning Using a Mind Map* Use a graphic organizer (mind map) to record reader's questions and answers	**Reading Strategy** *Synthesizing: Lessons Learned* Use pictures and words to explain something learned while reading the text	**Reading Strategy** *Connecting to Specific Facts* Identify facts and describe personal connections to these facts

Non-Fiction: Junior Grades

My Reading	Text Element	Word Skills	Taxonomy of Thinking
	Strengthening Understanding (junior) Explain how different text features strengthened understanding of text	*New To Me* Record new vocabulary. Illustrate and define	*Evaluating: Interesting Facts* Write three interesting facts and justify reader's choice
Reading Strategy *Questioning for Further Inquiry* Formulate questions for further research	**Reading Strategy** *Visualizing: Creating a Diagram* Create and label a diagram to demonstrate understanding	**Reading Strategy** *Determining Importance: Main Idea and Supporting Details* Identify main ideas and provide supporting details	**Reading Strategy** *Connecting to Previous Reading* Text-to-text: Describe connection to other texts

My Reading	Text Element	Word Skills	Taxonomy of Thinking
	Cover Information Use information on the front and back cover to formulate predictions	*Word Use* Use dictionary to find pronunciation and definition of new vocabulary. Write a sentence with new words.	*Analyzing: Fiction or Non-Fiction* Identify features of the text that demonstrate that it is non-fiction
Reading Strategy *Connecting Ideas within the Text* Use a Venn diagram to record similarities and differences between two main ideas within the same text	**Reading Strategy** *Questioning: FQR* Using facts from the text, form questions and consider responses	**Reading Strategy** *Determining Importance: Cause and Effect* Examine the cause and effect of main ideas from the text	**Reading Strategy** *Monitoring Understanding Using Rereading and Reading-on* Consider the effectiveness of rereading to repair comprehension

My Reading	Text Element *New Illustrations* Create four new illustrations to support the information in the text. Include captions for each illustration	Word Skills *Glossary* Create a glossary for new vocabulary	Taxonomy of Thinking *Analyzing: PMI Chart* Complete a PMI (Plus, Minus, Interesting) analysis for facts from the text
Reading Strategy *Connecting Using a Three-Part Diagram* Record a variety of connections to text	Reading Strategy *Synthesizing: "Hamburger" Paragraph* Write a paragraph summarizing one main idea and supporting details from the text	Reading Strategy *Determining Importance: Fact or Opinion* Record examples of facts and opinions from the text	Reading Strategy *Questioning Chart* Record prior knowledge and pose questions for further learning

Acknowledgments

As teachers, we are constantly evolving, changing, and adapting our teaching practice. I am fortunate to work in an amazing school board, where strong professional collaboration yields creative solutions and innovative teaching techniques. The board has formed networks intended for teachers to support and learn from each other. This book is the result of my participation in a number of these networks. Working with other teachers, consultants, and literacy experts has provided me with the opportunity to benefit greatly from the wealth of knowledge of other professionals.

Thanks to Michelle Sharratt for allowing me to visit her classroom years ago. The few hours I spent with her changed my teaching practice forever. Michelle introduced me to the concept of accountability tasks for independent reading in the form of 8-Boxes, which evolved through the years into this book. Barbara Harold assisted me with research and graphic organizers, and shared her wide range of expertise with me; thanks for the encouragement and gentle nudge to take small steps out of my comfort zone and into the unknown. Thank you to the entire staff and student body of O.M. MacKillop P.S.—What an amazing place to work and learn!—especially Yvonne West for demonstrating such amazing leadership, concern for students, and knowledge of literacy; Linda McVeigh for generously providing countless resources; Patty Cassels for her leadership in literacy; Mavis Bowden for reading passages of text and constantly cheering me on; and Lisa Gidlow, Sandy Jang, Lynn Allen, and Veni Bremner, who were eager to provide student samples to contribute to this publication. Thanks also to Ann Gnoinski and the staff and students at Brownridge P.S.—including Angie Braiantsis, Jordan Rappaport, Sandra Lostritto, and Mary MacKeracher —who piloted many of the reproducibles and provided valuable feedback. Thank you, Anne Porretta, for continuing to support me with my new adventures in literacy leadership and providing opportunities to share and refine my thinking. Thanks to Carol Matsoo for actively continuing to serve as my mentor and very trusted friend—your influence will remain with me my entire career.

Thanks to Kat Mototsune for helping me to strip the original draft of this manuscript to the bare bones and reinvent it as a focused, purposeful teaching tool. Thanks to Mary Macchiusi for encouraging me to write another book, and working so hard so that I could have my "perfect cover." Your support, encouragement, and clear direction make writing a pleasure. Thank you, Matthew W., for agreeing to be on the cover — an outstanding job!

Finally, thanks to my family: Mike, Matthew, and Hailey. Thanks, Mike, for doubling your parenting duties while I wrote and rewrote chunks of text, for sneaking snacks onto my desk without interrupting me while I was deep in thought, and for trying to sleep with the eerie glow of a computer and the constant clicking of the keys filling the room. Matthew and Hailey, thank you for your love and patience while I stole time away from you to write this book. I am so proud of all you do—keep drawing, writing, and reading.

References

Abromitis, B. (1994) "The Role of Metacognition in Reading Comprehension: Implications for Instruction" Literacy *Research and Reports*, Number 19

Anderson, Lorin W., Krathwohl, David R., et al. (eds.) (2001) *A Taxonomy for Learning, Teaching, and Assessing — A Revision of Bloom's Taxonomy of Educational Objectives*. New York, NY: Addison Wesley Longman, Inc.

Anderson, R.C., and Pearson, P.D. (1984) "A schema-theoretic view of basic reading processes" in P.D. Pearson (ed.), *Handbook of Reading Research*. New York, NY: Longman.

Anderson, R.C., Hiebert, E.H., Scott, A., and Wilkinson, I.A.G (1985) *Becoming a nation of readers: The report of the commission on Reading*. Washington, DC: National Institute of Education.

Beers, Kyleen (2003) *When Kids Can't Read: What Teachers Can Do*. Portsmouth, NH: Heinemann.

Bennett, B., and Rolheiser, C. (2001) *Beyond Monet, The Artful Science of Instructional Integration*. Toronto, ON: Bookation Inc.

Block, Cathy Collins, and Rodgers, Lori (2004) *Comprehension Process Instruction*. New York, NY: Guilford Press.

Booth, David (2002) *Even Hockey Players Read*. Markham, ON: Pembroke Publishers.

— (2007) *The Literacy Principal*. Markham, ON: Pembroke Publishers.

Boushey, Gail, and Moser, Joan (2006) *The Daily Five*. Portland, ME: Stenhouse Publishers.

Brown, A., Armbruster, B. B., and Baker, L. (1986) "The role of metacognition in reading and studying" 49–76 in J. Orasanu, *Reading comprehension: From research to practice* Hillsdale, NJ: Erlbaum.

Donohue, Lisa (2007) *Guided Listening*. Markham, ON: Pembroke Publishers.

Developmental Reading Assessment, Pearson Education

Fountas, Irene, and Pinnell, Gay Su (1996) *Guided Reading: Good First Teaching for All Children*. Portsmouth, NH: Heinemann.

— (2001) *Guiding Readers and Writers Grades 3–6: Teaching Comprehension, Genre, and Content Literacy*. Portsmouth, NH: Heinemann.

— (1999) *Matching Books to Readers: Using Leveled Books in Guided Reading, K – 3*. Portsmouth, NH: Heinemann.

Gear, Adrienne (2006) *Reading Power*. Markham, ON: Pembroke Publishers.

Harvey, Stephanie, and Goudvis, Anne (2007) *Strategies That Work: 2nd Edition*. Portland, ME: Stenhouse Publishers.

Israel, S., Block, C., Bauserman, K., and Kinnucan-Welsch, K. (2005) *Metacognition in Literacy Learning: Theory, Assessment, Instruction, and Professional Development*. Mahwah, NJ: Lawrence Erlbaum.

Katz, Claudia Anne, with Laura Polkoff and Debra Gurvitz. "'Shhh . . . I'm Reading': Scaffolded Independent-Level Reading" *School Talk* 10.2 (January 2005): 1-3.

Miller, Debbie (2002) *Reading With Meaning: Teaching Comprehension in the Primary Grades*. Portland, ME: Stenhouse.

Ontario Ministry of Education (1999) *The Ontario Curriculum – Exemplars Grades 1 – 8: Writing*

— (2000) *The Ontario Curriculum – Exemplars Grades 1 – 8: Reading*

— (2006) *The Ontario Curriculum: Grades 1 – 8: Language*

Palinscar A. S., and Ransom, K. (1988) "From the mystery spot to the thoughtful spot: The instruction of metacognitive strategies" *The Reading Teacher*, 41, 784–789.

Pressley, Michael (2000) *What Should Comprehension Instruction be the Instruction of?* as cited in: Barr, R, Pearson, D., Kamil, M.L., and Mosenthal, P. *Handbook of Reading Research*. Mahwah, NJ: Lawrence Erlbaum.

Pressley, Michael (2002) *Metacogntion and Self-Regulated Comprehension* as cited in Farstrup, Alan E., and Samuels, S. Jay *What Research Has to Say About Reading Instruction, Third Edition*. International Reading Association.

Routman, Regie (2003) *Reading Essentials: The Specifics You Need to Teach Reading Well*. Portsmouth, NH: Heinemann.

Rowling, J.K. (2007) *Harry Potter and the Deathly Hallows*. London, UK: Bloomsbury.

Stead, Tony (2006) *Reality Checks: Teaching Reading Comprehension with Nonfiction K–5*. Portland, ME: Stenhouse Publishers.

Taylor, B.M., Frye, B.J., and Maruyama, G.M. (1990) "Time spent reading and reading growth" *American Educational Research Journal*, 27, 351–362.

Tovani, Cris (2004) *Do I Really Have to Teach Reading?* Portland, ME: Stenhouse Publishers.

Trehearne, Miriam P. (2006) *Comprehensive Literacy Resource for Grades 3–6 Teachers*. Toronto, ON: Nelson.

www.hishelpinschool.com *Applying Bloom's Taxonomy to Teaching and Testing*

York Region District School Board, Curriculum and Instructional Services (2003) *English As a Second Language (ESL)/English Literacy Development (ELD) MEDIA KITS: A Teacher's Guide*

Index